LOOKING FOR LINCOLN IN ILLINOIS

LOOKING FOR LINCOLN IN ILLINOIS

LINCOLN'S SPRINGFIELD

Bryon C. Andreasen

Southern Illinois University Press
Carbondale

Cover illustrations (clockwise from top left): Abraham Lincoln,
    candidate for president, 1860, *also appears on title page*, (the
    Abraham Lincoln Presidential Library and the Illinois Historic
    Preservation Agency [ALPL/IHPA]); state outline by Tom
    Willcockson; Old State Capitol (ALPL/IHPA); mid-19th-century
    campaign apron (ALPL/IHPA); newspaper notice from 1860
    presidential campaign (*Illinois State Journal*, August 9, 1860);
    Sangamon County Courthouse (*left*) and Springfield Marine
    & Fire Insurance Company as seen from the Old State Capitol
    cupola (ALPL/IHPA); fireman using speaking trumpet to
    communicate over din at fire scene (ALPL/IHPA)

Library of Congress Cataloging-in-Publication Data
Andreasen, Bryon C.
Looking for Lincoln in Illinois : Lincoln's Springfield /
    Bryon C. Andreasen
    pages cm
Includes bibliographical references and index.
ISBN 978-0-8093-3382-0 (pbk. : alk. paper)
ISBN 0-8093-3382-1 (pbk. : alk. paper)
ISBN 978-0-8093-3383-7 (ebook)
ISBN 0-8093-3383-X (ebook)
1. Lincoln, Abraham, 1809–1865—Homes and haunts—Illinois—
    Springfield—Anecdotes. 2. Lincoln, Abraham, 1809–1865—
    Friends and associates—Anecdotes. 3. Springfield (Ill.)—Social
    life and customs—19th century—Anecdotes. 4. Springfield
    (Ill.)—History—19th century—Anecdotes. 5. Springfield (Ill.)—
    Buildings, structures, etc.—Anecdotes. I. Title.
F549.S7A29 2015
977.3'56 dc23   2014031069

*For Nicky Stratton, without whom there would
have been no Looking for Lincoln*

CONTENTS

Foreword   ix
Guy C. Fraker

Preface   xi

FOREWORD

Here I have lived a quarter of a century and have passed from a
young to an old man.
                    —Abraham Lincoln, February 11, 1861

FEW AMERICANS HAVE DEMONSTRATED THE COMBINATION OF

ambition and selflessness, integrity and pragmatism, confidence and humility, and persistent pursuit of that which is right as did Abraham Lincoln. It is one of those incredibly fortunate instances in our history where the right man was there at the right time. Lincoln understood, as perhaps no one else, the stakes in the Civil War. It was not merely the Union at stake; it was also the very institution of democracy. Where did he get the qualities and skills it took to steer the nation and democracy through this crisis?

The major portion of his training for this task was in central Illinois. Little has been written about his life and development from when he arrived in the year of his 21st birthday until his departure for the White House 31 years later. The frontier of central Illinois was the perfect place for this rawboned farm-hand to hone his natural talent and intellectual skills to meet the challenges that the nation would face.

Lincoln and the region evolved on parallel courses, maturing together. The coming of the railroads some 20 years after his arrival totally changed the region. He learned to deal with change and the revolutionary transformation of society that took place there in the 1850s. He traveled extensively across the region, first by horse and then by train, practicing law and pursuing politics. There are numerous sites, buildings, homes, streetscapes, and landscapes in the towns that he visited and the prairies that he crossed. This region felt the presence and influence of Lincoln. It, in turn, influenced and molded him.

An in-depth understanding of this enigmatic, iconic figure cannot be reached without becoming acquainted with the region and Lincoln's role in it. The political and social forces of the era made Illinois a key state in the 1850s. At that time, central Illinois was the state's most vital area. Lincoln gained the Republican nomination for president because he built the network to do so while traveling central Illinois.

The Abraham Lincoln National Heritage Area was created by Congress in 2008 and is affiliated with the National Park Service. The Area preserves the life and times of Abraham Lincoln in central Illinois. This 42-county area is a nationally significant landscape and network of sites associated with the social, cultural, economic, and political complexities of the antebellum period of our nation's history. The Looking for Lincoln Heritage Coalition coordinates projects, programs, and events that focus on telling the unique stories of the Area, enhancing and promoting Lincoln scholarship, heritage tourism, and stimulating economic development within the region.

This effort includes the publication of a shelf of books examining Lincoln's development and rise during his time in central Illinois. It is our intent that these publications will enhance the Looking for Lincoln Heritage Coalition's efforts to

- create engaging experiences that connect places and stories throughout the heritage area and promote public awareness of the region's history, culture, and significance;
- promote heritage, cultural, and recreational tourism and related heritage development that support increased economic activity and investment in heritage resources; and
- raise public consciousness about the needs and benefits of preserving the historic and cultural legacies of central Illinois.

It is my hope that you are inspired to learn more about the life, times, and legacy of Abraham Lincoln in central Illinois and the people, places, and forces in the region that shaped and elevated him to the White House.

Guy C. Fraker
Chairman of the Looking for Lincoln Heritage Coalition

PREFACE

THE ABRAHAM LINCOLN PRESIDENTIAL LIBRARY AND MUSEUM

is a great starting place to begin exploring the life and times of America's greatest president. But it is only that . . . a *starting* place. Beyond the museum's walls lies the physical landscape where the people of Lincoln's generation actually experienced their lives. That landscape, however, with a few exceptions, has changed significantly since Lincoln's time, making it difficult for people today to imagine Lincoln's world.

To help visitors exercise their historical imaginations, the Looking for Lincoln Heritage Coalition decided to create a network of wayside storyboards. The initial phase was to focus on downtown Springfield—the center of Lincoln's adult life in Illinois. I was assigned to research and write storyboards for downtown Springfield that could be a kind of outdoor extension of the Presidential Museum and become a model for storyboard programs in other localities.

It took careful research to identify the physical locations where various Lincoln-related stories occurred. From a list of over sixty possible story locations, I chose fifty sites and wrote story texts for them. I did not write stories for the well-known sites that still survive from Lincoln's time and that are open and interpreted for visitors—the Lincoln Home, the Old State Capitol, the Lincoln-Herndon Law Offices, and the Lincoln Tomb. Nevertheless, each of these major historic sites is referenced herein as part of the story of a lesser-known site.

In conceptualizing each storyboard, I followed a dual-story theme: one story focusing on Lincoln the person, and the other focusing on the Springfield world that Lincoln knew—"Springfield's Lincoln" and "Lincoln's Springfield," if you will. This approach enriches the visitor experience by incorporating aspects of social and cultural history into the stories.

Repeated requests for copies of the storyboard texts in part prompted the production of this book. Included are all fifty texts written for Springfield's initial wayside program (including texts for twelve storyboards that were not produced). The stories need not be read in any particular order, nor in extended sittings. Rather, they can be sampled and enjoyed severally as time permits.

For those who have visited Springfield and encountered some of the storyboards, I hope the book will serve as a fond reminder of what I trust was a pleasant and stimulating visit to the Land of Lincoln's capital city. For those who have not visited, I hope it will generate the interest to do so.

I acknowledge all my former colleagues at the Abraham Lincoln Presidential Library whose assistance made the original wayside program (and, hence, this book) possible.

Bryon C. Andreasen

LOOKING FOR LINCOLN IN ILLINOIS

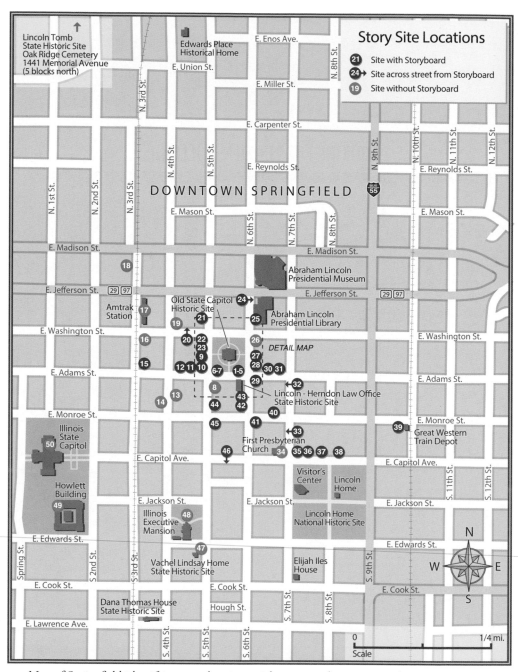

Lincoln Tomb
State Historic Site
Oak Ridge Cemetery
1441 Memorial Avenue
(5 blocks north)

Edwards Place
Historical Home

E. Enos Ave.

E. Union St.

E. Miller St.

E. Carpenter St.

E. Reynolds St.

N. 8th St.

E. Reynolds St.

DOWNTOWN SPRINGFIELD

BUS 55

E. Mason St.

E. Mason St.

E. Madison St.

E. Madison St.

Abraham Lincoln
Presidential Museum

18

E. Jefferson St. 29 97

E. Jefferson St. 29 97

Amtrak
Station

17

Old State Capitol
Historic Site **24**➜

Abraham Lincoln
Presidential Library

25

E. Washington St.

19

21

E. Washington St.

16

20 **22**

23

9

26

DETAIL MAP

E. Adams St.

15

12 **11** **10**

6-7 **1-5**

27

28

30 **31**

E. Adams St.

8

29

Lincoln - Herndon Law Office
State Historic Site

32

E. Monroe St.

14

13

44

43

42

40

39

Great Western
Train Depot

E. Monroe St.

Illinois
State
Capitol

50

45

41

33

First Presbyterian
Church **34** **35** **36** **37** **38**

E. Capitol Ave.

46

Visitor's
Center

Lincoln
Home

E. Capitol Ave.

S. 11th St.

S. 12th St.

Howlett
Building

49

E. Jackson St.

E. Jackson St.

Lincoln Home
National Historic Site

E. Jackson St.

Illinois
Executive
Mansion **48**

E. Edwards St.

Vachel Lindsay Home
State Historic Site **47**

Elijah Iles
House

E. Edwards St.

N

W   E

S

E. Cook St.

E. Cook St.

E. Cook St.

Dana Thomas House
State Historic Site

Hough St.

S. 7th St.

S. 8th St.

S. 9th St.

E. Lawrence Ave.

Spring St.

S. 2nd St.

S. 3rd St.

S. 4th St.

S. 5th St.

S. 6th St.

N. 1st St.

N. 2nd St.

N. 3rd St.

N. 4th St.

N. 5th St.

N. 6th St.

N. 7th St.

N. 8th St.

N. 9th St.

N. 10th St.

N. 11th St.

N. 12th St.

0   1/4 mi.

Scale

Map of Springfield identifying story locations with corresponding story numbers

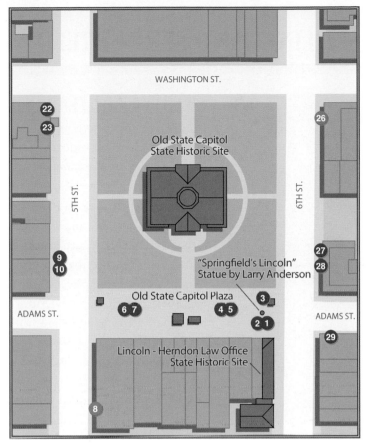

Enlarged map of the central block around the Old State Capitol public square

Story Site Locations

Lincoln's earliest known photograph, circa 1846, at about age 37—"No wealthy or popular relations to recommend me"

TWENTY-EIGHT-YEAR-OLD

Abraham Lincoln settled here in 1837. He was unmarried, unlearned, unrefined, with *"no wealthy or popular relations to recommend me."* On the day before his fifty-second birthday, Lincoln left here a profoundly changed man: a husband and father, financially secure, his intellectual and moral capacities having grown to match his towering physical stature; his deeply held political convictions tempered by empathy and keen insight into the human condition. On this public square and in surrounding buildings, Lincoln and his family and friends purchased goods, attended parties, enjoyed picnics and parades, watched theatricals, and listened to concerts and lectures. In law offices and courtrooms overlooking this square he honed his skills of persuasion. In storefront discussions and street corner gatherings he perfected the art of politics. Then, as his understanding matured and his convictions deepened, he took his place among the leaders of his time, addressing the people of the nation in powerful and eloquent words that echoed beyond this small prairie capital.

SPRINGFIELD WAS THE CENTER

of Lincoln's world for a quarter century. When he arrived here Springfield was, like himself, shaking off its rough, frontier beginnings. The legislature had recently named it the state capital—but there was no statehouse. Fewer than two thousand people lived here. In summer the unpaved streets were dusty, and in winter they were hopelessly muddy. Cows, chickens, and pigs wandered freely about, frogs croaked in undrained swamps. To the unsophisticated Lincoln, however, Springfield had more grandeur than the backwoods settlements from whence he came. As Lincoln grew in ecotnomic status and social position, so too did his city. When Lincoln left in February 1861 to assume the presidency, Springfield had almost 10,000 inhabitants and boasted of many impressive buildings and social institutions. Neither Lincoln nor his city was "frontier" anymore.

Lincoln's last Springfield photograph, taken February 9, 1861, as President-elect, three days shy of his 52nd birthday—a man shaped by lessons in practical democracy and human nature learned "in this place" and among "these people"

Washington Street in Springfield as Lincoln knew it, looking west to the railroad crossing at Third Street

This picture of Lincoln at age 45 is his second-earliest known photograph. It was taken in October 1854 in Chicago just three weeks after he gave his stirring antislavery speech in Springfield's Old State Capitol.

THE YEAR 1854 MARKED

Lincoln's public return to politics following a five-year hiatus. That year Senator Stephen A. Douglas of Illinois pushed the Kansas-Nebraska Act through the U.S. Congress, overturning the 1820 Missouri Compromise line. Fearing the spread of slavery to western territories, Abraham Lincoln was aroused *"as he had never been before."* Contemporaries considered the speech he delivered here in the Old State Capital on October 4, 1854, to be *"one of the ablest & most effective of his life,"* and identified this as *"the occasion of his becoming a great antislavery leader."* Lincoln spoke for three hours, proclaiming, *"[M]y ancient faith teaches me that 'all men are created equal'; and that there can be no moral right in connection with one man's making a slave of another."* Republican newspapers boasted that Douglas had never before endured *"such a remorseless tearing of his flimsy arguments."* Lincoln repeated the speech in Peoria two weeks later, and it has come down in history as the Peoria Speech. Historians consider it to be one of Lincoln's most significant addresses.

Mary was age 36 in 1854. There is no known photo of her from that year. Mary did not like to have her picture taken. She thought photos made her hands too large and her features too fat. Here she appears in 1860 at age 42.

MARY LINCOLN WAS HEARD TO

scold her husband, *"Why don't you dress up and look like somebody?"* Mary was a well-bred daughter of Kentucky aristocrats. Abraham was the rough son of illiterate Kentucky dirt farmers. So it is not surprising that Mary tried to educate Lincoln in matters of proper dress and social behavior. The first big purchase of their marriage was "superior black cloth" for a man's suit! She provided what her biographer described as *"a marriage-long course in middle-class etiquette."*

In Mary's time, women were expected to be the family's guardian of morality and Christian conduct. Gentrifying her husband conformed to Mary's expected marital role. Unlike conventional political wives of her day, however, Mary was openly ambitious for her husband's success and assertive in giving him political advice. The recipient of much criticism, Mary paid a price for being ahead of her time.

Artist Larry Anderson's statue grouping, titled "Springfield's Lincoln," portrays Mary Lincoln adjusting her husband's tie as he prepares to enter the Old State Capitol to deliver his important address.

The Old State Capitol is where Lincoln delivered his October 4, 1854, address. Four years later, he delivered his "House Divided Speech" there, and in 1865 his body lay in state there for the last time before burial. Today it is open to visitors as a state historic site administered by the Illinois Historic Preservation Agency.

This Christmas advertisement from an 1854 Springfield newspaper gave children a powerful incentive to be "good Boys and Girls." Watson's was on the South side of the public square.

THE SPRINGFIELD "URBAN"

environment that shaped the childhood of the Lincoln boys was a far cry from the "backwoods" wilderness their father knew as a child. "Pay schools" and academies, railroad trains and fancy carriages, circuses and Sunday schools, hardware stores and drug store candies—this was indeed a different world from the rough frontier of previous generations. Though more urbane, Springfield was not necessarily a safer environment for children. *"Our city is in an extremely filthy condition,"* complained a resident. *"Backyards, necessaries, ponds with putrid waters, can be seen all about."* In 1850 (the year Lincoln's almost four-year-old son Eddie died), one-half of all Springfield deaths were children under five. Citizens also believed that Springfield had a serious "boy problem." An 8 P.M. curfew prohibited boys from raiding orchards, exploding firecrackers, beating each other, *"making a noise or creating any disturbance,"* or otherwise engaging in *"malicious mischief."* Punishment was a day in jail. Still, it was commonly reported that *"boys from ten to fourteen years old [are] perambulating our streets after 12 o'clock at night."*

There is no known undisputed photo of Edward Baker "Eddie" Lincoln, who died about a month before his fourth birthday in 1850.

THE LINCOLN BOYS IN 1854

One-year-old Tad was too young to attend activities. Four-year-old Willie—considered bright and gentle-mannered—shared his father's tastes and talents. Eddie had died four years earlier, leaving a seven-year gap between 11-year-old Robert and Willie. This contributed to the distance that seemed to separate Robert from the rest of the family. He resented his parents' indulgence of his younger brothers. As the oldest, he paid an emotional price for Lincoln's frequent absences from home. More than the others, he absorbed the aristocratic attitudes of his mother's family, and may have felt that his father was "inferior." In 1854 Robert attended preparatory school in Springfield. Mary boasted of his learning Latin and Greek, but Robert later conceded *we did just what pleased us, study consuming only a very small portion of our time.*

Thomas "Tad" Lincoln

William Wallace "Willie" Lincoln

Willie and Tad running wild in their father's law office in a scene from the Abraham Lincoln Presidential Museum

Robert Todd Lincoln

4. SAMUEL S. BALL'S
BATH & BARBER SHOP

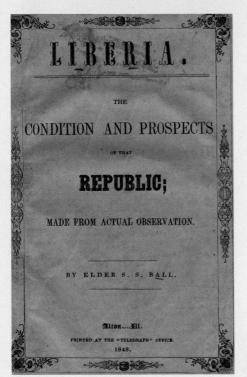

LIBERIA.

THE

CONDITION AND PROSPECTS

OF THAT

REPUBLIC;

MADE FROM ACTUAL OBSERVATION.

BY ELDER S. S. BALL.

Alton....Ill.

PRINTED AT THE "TELEGRAPH" OFFICE.
1848.

Although he usually patronized another African American Springfield barber, Abraham Lincoln shared Samuel Ball's attitudes toward voluntary colonization for American blacks.

"THE BATHING ROOMS NOW KEPT *by Rev. S. S. Ball in the rear of his Barber's Shop are in elegant trim for the accommodation of his friends and the public,"* advertised Elder Ball. His shop was on the south side of the public square (1849–1852). He also sold "Ball's Restorative" to prevent baldness. But the Rev. Ball's true passion was the betterment of his people. As an agent for the Colored Baptist Association he traveled to Africa in 1848 to evaluate Liberia as an *"asylum for free blacks."* He later championed colonization—believing that black people could practice democracy and prosper economically in Liberia free from white oppression. He petitioned the Illinois legislature to finance emigration, but he died of typhoid fever at age 42—his plans unfulfilled. Many of Springfield's African Americans did not share their minister's dream. Black Springfield residents held an anticolonization rally in Clinton Hall on the north side of the square a few months before the Lincoln-Douglas debates in 1858.

PEOPLE DID NOT BATHE MUCH

in Lincoln's day. Many did not consider
being dirty as degrading. Churches, however, began teaching that cleanliness was a
moral requirement. And social reformers
taught that it was necessary for respectability. Still, social commitment to cleanliness
took time. Not until the 1850s did regular
personal washing become routine for
many Americans. By then many bedrooms
had basins, pitchers, and washstands (but
not tubs). An 1851 plan to put a bathroom
in the White House was widely denounced
as an "unnecessary expense." Bath soap
became a middle-class standard sometime
around the Civil War. By 1860 Boston had
3,910 bathtubs for a population of 177,840.
New York's capital, Albany, reported just
19 tubs. The 1860 newspapers in Illinois'
capital occasionally advertised bathtubs
or public bathing facilities. Only a few
barbers and hotels had public baths.

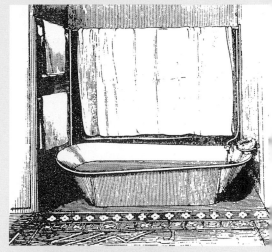

*Social reformers encouraged more
frequent bathing.*

*Fish Town at Bassau, by Robert K. Griffin, a mid-nineteenth-century watercolor of the coast
of Liberia, the African country that the Rev. Ball visited to evaluate colonization.*

5. C. M. & S. SMITH STORE

Clark M. Smith accompanied Mary Lincoln to New York City in January 1861 to help her pick fashions that would be socially acceptable in Washington, D.C.

SHOPPERS AT CLARK M. SMITH'S

all-purpose store on the south side of the public square seldom paid cash. Money was scarce; credit accounts were common. Smith's in-laws—the Lincolns—had an account. After her husband lost the Senate race to Stephen Douglas, Mary Lincoln launched into a therapeutic spending spree, buying silk and fancy trimmings for a new dress. Routine purchases included boots and hats, chickens and eggs, pocket knives and wood, salt for making ice cream, cinnamon and sugar—lots of sugar! At the time sugar was touted as the "most nourishing substance in nature." Mary certainly "nourished" her family. At one point she had charges for 32 pounds of

Clark Smith's store was one of several located along the public square around the capitol building.

regular sugar, six pounds of crushed sugar, and two gallons of syrup. Lincoln usually settled his store account several times a year. But others didn't. The year Lincoln ran for president, Smith announced he would no longer keep accounts for customers. Henceforth his store would be "An Exclusively Cash and Produce Business."

AS PRESIDENT-ELECT, LINCOLN

found it difficult to get away from the press of well-wishers and office seekers. Desperate to find a place where he could work undisturbed on his important First Inaugural Address, he received permission from his brother-in-law to use a back room on the third floor of the store. On the sloping front of a merchant's desk, hidden away from Springfield's bustling public square, Lincoln drafted the first version of what, in its final form, became a plea to our *"better angels"*—applicable in all times and places: *"Why should there not be a patient confidence in the ultimate justice of the people? . . . We are not enemies, but friends. We must not be enemies. Though passion may have strained, it must not break our bonds of affection. . . ."*

The desk and the inkwell that Lincoln used while drafting his First Inaugural Address are in the Abraham Lincoln Presidential Library collection.

Dr. Amos W. French

DR. A. W. FRENCH,

SURGEON DENTIST.

OFFICE:

SOUTH-WEST CORNER OF THE PUBLIC SQUARE,

SPRINGFIELD, ILL.

Amos W. French, Lincoln's dentist, had offices in the Bunn Building on the southwest corner of the public square.

AMERICANS HAD POOR ORAL

hygiene in Lincoln's era. Rotted teeth and foul breath were common (halitosis was not yet a social evil). Calomel frequently prescribed by doctors for fevers caused many people to have loose teeth. Dentistry was plagued by ignorance and quackery. Barbers were the usual practitioners of tooth extraction, wielding the dreaded "turn-key" used to twist out stubborn teeth. Various craftsmen tinkered at creating dentures, including carved ivory, metal plates that occasionally featured old sheep's teeth, or even hickory plugs soaked in creosote. After Dr. Amos W. French arrived from New York in 1848, he soon acquired a reputation as one of the best "mechanical dentists" in the West. He was also a book collector; his upper-floor office looked more like a library than a dentist's office. He and Lincoln studied German together—but Lincoln kept the class in turmoil with his storytelling. After the Civil War, French participated in the scientific revolution that transformed the dental profession.

LINCOLN HAD A BAD EXPERIENCE WITH A DENTIST BEFORE DR. FRENCH

arrived. In an 1841 letter, he wrote about having a painful tooth extracted: *"I had it torn out, bringing with it a bit of the jawbone; the consequence of which is that my mouth is now so sore that I can neither talk, nor eat."* An 1843 store account shows that Lincoln bought a toothbrush. Perhaps this reflects Mary's refining influence. As president, he took precautions when visiting the dentist, for he reportedly took along a small bottle of chloroform to help deaden the pain of having a tooth pulled. When the doctor approached with forceps, Lincoln surprised him by administering the analgesic to himself before allowing the doctor to proceed. The practice of analgesia in dentistry was not common at the time.

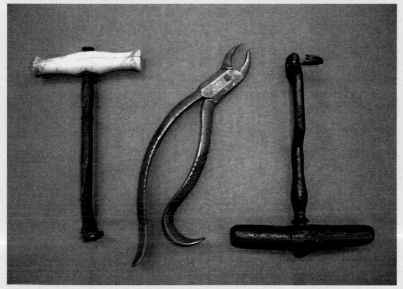

Dental instruments of the period included "turn-keys"—pictured on both the left and right.

The enterprising Curran once attracted curious costumers by displaying a Japanese coin in his store.

THE GREGARIOUS GENERAL ISAAC

B. Curran was a prominent citizen in Lincoln's Springfield. His store on the south side of the square was a popular gathering place for Lincoln's political opponents. Curran arrived as a young silversmith from Ithaca, New York, in 1840. He worked at Chatterton's for several years (where he supposedly engraved Mary's wedding ring), before setting up his own shop in competition with his former employers. Curran was married only a year when his young bride died. He did not remarry for twenty-five years, living much of that time in the rooms above his store. He fell in with Stephen Douglas and became his Springfield point man whenever the famous senator attended Congress. One Democratic governor appointed him quartermaster general; another made him chief of staff. He lost his appointment as a federal pension official when Douglas had a falling out with President James Buchanan. Lincoln appointed Curran to a wartime diplomatic post in Germany.

HAIR BRAIDING BECAME AN IMPORTANT ART IN MAKING CERTAIN

jewelry items in Lincoln's era. Elaborate hair wreaths were hung on walls to memorialize loved ones. Brooches and funeral jewelry made from the hair of the deceased became common aspects of Victorian mourning customs. In 1860 Curran hired a Miss Summers—a *"celebrated hair braider"*—to work in his store. *"Hitherto persons requiring such work have been compelled to send the hair to New York,"* Curran noted. *"Now it can be done here at a great saving of cost."* Miss Summers boasted of 280 patterns embracing breast-pins, earrings, bracelets, fob-chains, watch guards, and finger rings. Curran promised that his *"good taste, aided by that of the artiste, will insure the most graceful and fashionable work."*

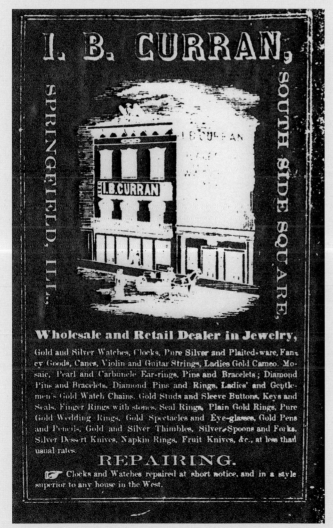

An 1857 store advertisement for Curran's store

8. LINCOLN'S INVENTION

LINCOLN'S GENERATION WITNESSED A TIME OF GREAT

engineering curiosity and inventiveness. Previous generations had for centuries experienced little change in the material conditions of average people. That changed in America during Lincoln's lifetime. Technical innovations in transportation, communication, agriculture, and manufacturing accelerated the pace of change in everyday life. American inventions between 1830 and 1860 included the first American-built railroad locomotive, the mechanical reaper, repeating pistols, the self-scouring steel plow, vulcanized rubber, the introduction of ether in surgery, the telegraph, sewing machines, rotary printing presses, elevators, and the first American oil well, to name just a few.

In his lecture "Discoveries and Inventions" Lincoln identified "Patent laws" as critical to promoting innovation by giving "the fuel of interest to the fire of genius." He wished to encourage the spirit of invention, and was involved in several patent cases as a lawyer. He is the only American president to have patented an invention—patent no. 6469. The patent model for his invention is in the Smithsonian Institution in Washington, D.C. It is not surprising that as president during the Civil War he pushed hard for new developments in weapons technology.

Lincoln reflected the spirit of his times in his affinity for mechanical things. His penchant for machines influenced his legal practice, as well. *"He had great Mechanical genius,"* a legal colleague recalled. *"[He] could understand readily the principles & mechanical action of machinery, & had the power, in his clear, simple illustrations & Style to make the jury comprehend them."*

DURING NOVEMBER 1848 LINCOLN WORKED DILIGENTLY TO CONSTRUCT

a working scale model of his invention for floating steamboats over shallow river shoals by inflating buoyant canvas chambers designed to lift boats over obstacles. He worked in his friend Walter Davis's cabinet shop located on the east side of Fifth Street. Sometimes he carried the model to his law office where he whittled on it and extolled its virtues to his law partner, William Herndon. When Lincoln returned to Washington, D.C., for his final session of Congress he filed for a patent, which was granted on May 22, 1849. He reportedly demonstrated a four-foot-long model for curious onlookers in the water trough on the southeast corner of the public square. Most were impressed. Herndon was not, observing that the apparatus had *"never been put on any boat so far as known."*

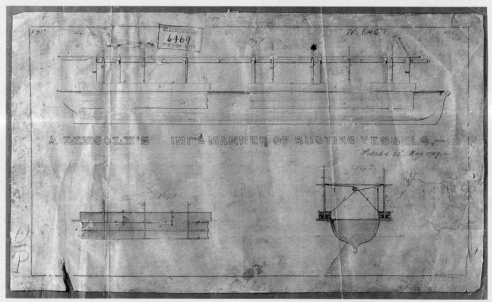

Lincoln's patent design drawings

9. MARY LINCOLN'S WEDDING RING

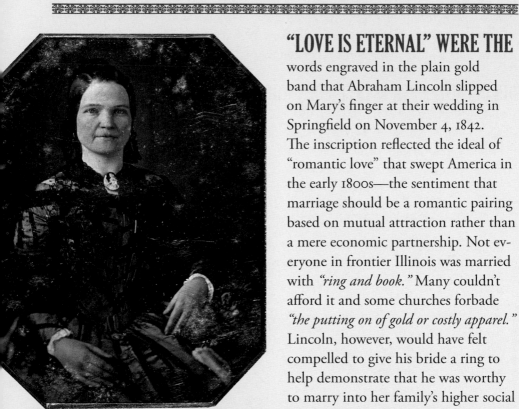

"LOVE IS ETERNAL" WERE THE words engraved in the plain gold band that Abraham Lincoln slipped on Mary's finger at their wedding in Springfield on November 4, 1842. The inscription reflected the ideal of "romantic love" that swept America in the early 1800s—the sentiment that marriage should be a romantic pairing based on mutual attraction rather than a mere economic partnership. Not everyone in frontier Illinois was married with *"ring and book."* Many couldn't afford it and some churches forbade *"the putting on of gold or costly apparel."* Lincoln, however, would have felt compelled to give his bride a ring to help demonstrate that he was worthy to marry into her family's higher social class. Mary's wedding band was still on her finger when she was buried in the Lincoln Tomb in 1882. Abraham Lincoln apparently never had a wedding ring; it was not yet customary. None of his pictures show him wearing a ring.

The close-up from Mary's earliest photograph, taken in 1846, shows her wedding band— a rare view since she usually wore gloves for photographs.

TRADITION HOLDS THAT

Chatterton's Jewelry Store is where Lincoln bought Mary's wedding ring. In 1842 Charles and George Chatterton—natives of Ithaca, New York—were young men in their twenties. They became prosperous merchants. George built a "castle cottage" home with towers and embattlements on "Aristocracy Hill" on the south side of town. A fire destroyed the store in 1853, but George rebuilt it, installing a sundial in the back so that townspeople could correctly set their timepieces. By the time Lincoln was elected president in 1860 Chatterton's was selling sheet music, pianos, melodeons, and other instruments, as well as jewelry and watches. During the Civil War Lincoln appointed Charles as Indian agent for the Cherokees.

Chatterton's Jewelry Store was a fixture on the west side of the public square in Lincoln's Springfield.

The Reverend Charles Dresser married the Lincolns in a ring ceremony. Two years later the couple bought Dresser's home on Eighth and Jackson Streets in Springfield.

10. LINCOLN'S HAT

1862 photograph of Lincoln in a stovepipe hat at Antietam Battlefield. Few photographs exist of Lincoln wearing a hat. All were taken in the field with Union soldiers—none in Illinois.

LINCOLN REPORTEDLY HAD A *"very defective taste"* in hats. At various times he was known to have worn fur caps, straw or palm hats, and broad, low-brimmed wool or felt hats. He is best known for the "plug" or stovepipe hats he wore as a lawyer and as president. *"His hat was brown and faded and the nap invariably worn or rubbed off,"* a friend remembered. Another complained that Lincoln's tall hat *"was not always exquisitely groomed"*—that it settled heavily on top of his wide ears. Another said that the hat Lincoln wore at the Lincoln-Douglas debates was *"much worse for wear."* Perhaps this was because Lincoln habitually used his hat as a desk and filing cabinet—stuffing letters, legal papers, and scribbled speech notes inside it. This was not always wise. As a Congressman attending the 1849 inauguration of President Zachary Taylor, Lincoln supposedly had his hat stolen—losing whatever literary treasures were inside it!

HATS WERE IMPORTANT TO MEN IN LINCOLN'S DAY. ALL MEN AND

boys wore them. Americans in the mid-19th century sported a wide variety of caps and hats. A friend of Lincoln's stated, *"Hats are the item of dress that does more than any other for the improvement of one's personal appearance."* Hats also marked a man's social status. Working men wore soft felt hats of every shape. Cloth railroad caps were also popular. Young men and boys liked dark wool sea caps with leather bills. Stiff felt bowlers and silk (replacing beaver) stovepipes adorned upper-middle-class business-men. George Hall, who in 1860 ran a haberdashery shop on the west side of the square, is said to have made one of the stovepipe hats that Lincoln wore.

Photographer Mathew Brady made this picture of Tad Lincoln with his sea cap in 1861.

> ☞ Lincoln is not in favor of the people making their own laws.
>
> ## PEOPLE OF SANGAMON
>
> ### REMEMBER,
>
> ## A VOTE FOR COOK AND BROWN
>
> IS A VOTE FOR
>
> ## LINCOLN AND NEGRO EQUALITY!
>
> VOTE FOR
>
> ## BARRET AND SHORT,
>
> AND SUSTAIN
>
> # DOUGLAS
>
> —AND—
>
> ## POPULAR RIGHTS!
>
> ☞ If you want to give countenance to the doctrine of negro-equality, and think that a negro is as good as a white man, politically and socially,— vote for Lincoln representatives.

November 1858 Register notices, one published on Election Day and the other (opposite page) *the day after— documenting the end of the heated and hectic Lincoln-Douglas senatorial contest.*

WHEN THE SEAT OF GOVERNMENT left Vandalia in 1839, the former capital's Democratic newspaper—the *Illinois State Register*—followed. Its offices were on the north side of Adams Street. *Register* editors William Walters and George Weber—and later, George Walker and Charles Lanphier—lived in a time when editors defended their views with their fists. The sheriff once horse-whipped Weber for printing unflattering words; Weber's brother then knifed the sheriff (Stephen Douglas won his acquittal). Another time Walker and Lanphier got into a street fight with Lincoln's friend, Whig editor Simeon Francis. They employed walking sticks and pitchforks. During the Civil War, the *Register* rallied in defense of the Union but bitterly opposed Lincoln's war policies. In 1864 a riot broke out when a mob (including soldiers) broke all the *Register* office windows. Unbowed, the paper declared that *"a vote for Abraham Lincoln is a vote for war, for murder, for the impoverishment of our people . . . because he will not abate one jot of his determination . . . to wipe out slavery."*

CHARLES H. LANPHIER EDITED

the *Register* for 18 years. He grew up in
Washington, D.C., where his family ran
a boardinghouse on Pennsylvania Avenue
in the shadow of Andrew Jackson's White
House. At age 16 he came to Illinois to
work as a newspaper printer; by age 26 he
was sole owner of the *Register*. From his
Springfield editor's chair Lanphier became
one of the most powerful Democrats in
Illinois. He, along with most Democrats,
believed abolitionists were traitors and
their sentiments *"atrocious."* He strongly
condemned President Lincoln, charging
him with subverting the Constitution and
turning the Civil War into a violent social
revolution that *"the civilized world will
denounce as an ineffaceable disgrace to the
American name."* He sold the *Register* in
1863. In his later years he became a champion for Springfield's public schools.

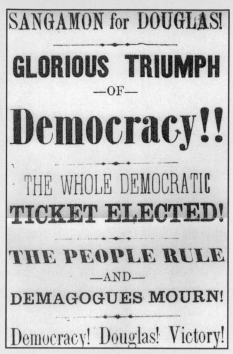

*November 1858 Register notices published
on Election Day* (opposite page) *and
the day after—documenting the end of
the heated and hectic Lincoln-Douglas
senatorial contest.*

*Newspaper editor Charles H. Lanphier was
an important voice for Illinois Democrats
who opposed Lincoln's policies during the
Civil War.*

12. CAMPAIGN POLES

CAMPAIGN POLES WERE A STAPLE OF POLITICAL CAMPAIGNS

in Lincoln's time. Democrats erected hickory poles—evoking party hero Andrew Jackson ("Old Hickory"). Whigs (and later Republicans) erected ash poles—honoring Henry Clay (whose estate was named "Ashland"). During the 1844 Clay-Polk presidential contest, Democrats erected a 150-foot-tall hickory pole in front of the *Register* office. On top was an American flag sewn by the Democratic ladies of Springfield. Party leaders encouraged young men to bring their *"sweethearts"* and old men their *"wives and daughters"* to the sunrise pole raising. Whigs scoffed that *"buzzards were observed . . . flying around in graceful circles some hundred feet above the pole."* They, in turn, raised a 214½-foot ash pole—the tallest in the nation—that weighed an estimated 22,000 pounds and took over two hours to raise. On the first attempt a guy rope broke and the pole fell, crushing one worker and crippling another. Whigs unjustly accused Democrats of cutting the rope.

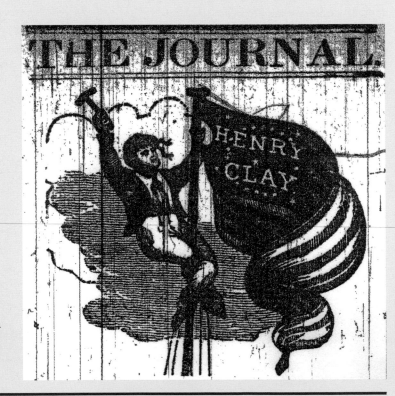

Lashed to Lincoln's 120-foot presidential ash pole in 1860 was a broom—signifying Lincoln's intent to sweep corrupt Democrats out of Washington's Augean stables.

CHILDREN ALSO PARTICIPATED IN LINCOLN-ERA POLITICS.

During the 1844 campaign, processions of Democratic boys and girls saluted cheering crowds at the hickory pole in front of the *Register* office on their way to visit Illinois' Democratic governor, Thomas Ford. *"It was beautiful to behold the youth of both sexes thus engaged so early in the cause of their country,"* gushed the *Register*'s editors. Ford proudly observed, *"Who knows but one of you may live to be President of these United States."* When Lincoln ran for president in 1860, children were part of the crowds inside the Republican "Wigwam," or convention center. During the Civil War, a group of Republican school children, aided by two soldiers, confronted a pistol-toting woman and tore down a Confederate flag that she had posted in front of her Springfield house.

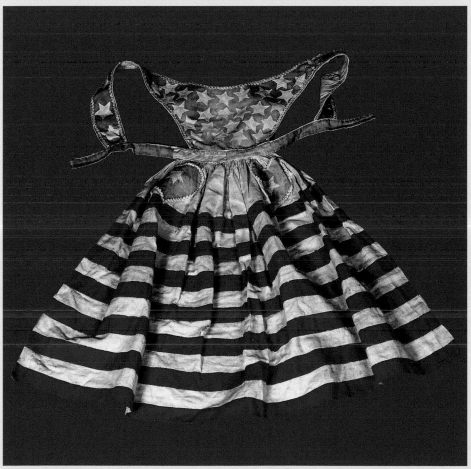

A mid-19th-century child's campaign apron from the Abraham Lincoln Presidential Library's collection

13. FOURTH STREET COTTAGE

"[T]HE PROPER WIDTH OF SIDE WALKS ON 4TH STREET"

was just one decision that Lincoln made as a town trustee (June 1839–April 1840). He could not have known that four years later he would live on the same street in a rented cottage with a young wife and toddler son. Serving for several months as one of Springfield's five governing trustees, 30-year-old bachelor Lincoln helped determine the local property tax rate, which streets and bridges to create or repair, and how to respond to citizens' petitions for a variety of ordinances—from abating "nuisances" (gambling, noisemaking, disorderliness, profane language) to awarding (or prohibiting) liquor licenses. At the same time Lincoln also served in the state legislature. There he oversaw

FIRST-HOME OF MR & MRS A. LINCOLN
-1843-44- SPRINGFIELD, ILL.

COMPLIMENTS OF
HARRY J. REIGER
ARCHITECT

The Lincolns rented a small cottage at 214 South Fourth Street in the autumn of 1843, several months after the first birthday of their son Robert. It consisted of three rooms— two fronting the street and a kitchen "L" in the rear. Small frame houses like this were standard for Springfield's clerks, artisans, and mechanics. The Lincolns lived here less than a year, moving again in May 1844 after they purchased a home on Jackson Street (the current Lincoln Home National Historic Site).

a bill to transform Springfield into a fully chartered city. Democrats opposed the charter because it permitted only Springfield citizens to vote, excluding aliens such as Irish railroad workers who tended to vote Democratic. Despite muddy street scuffles between opposing politicians, the charter bill passed and Springfield became the fourth incorporated city in Illinois—ending Lincoln's brief career in town government.

IT MAY HAVE BEEN HERE THAT

Abraham Lincoln first met his father-in-law, Robert S. Todd of Lexington, Kentucky. Todd came in the autumn of 1843 to visit family and to meet his namesake grandson, Robert Lincoln. He also undoubtedly checked on the progress of a lawsuit that his son-in-law was handling for him (*Todd v. Ware.*). Todd attempted to pay for Springfield-area land with devalued Illinois State Bank notes. The seller refused to accept them. Lincoln argued that by contract the seller was bound to accept the notes. But he lost the case. Todd completed the purchase with higher-valued Missouri banknotes, instead. He then divided the land among several family members, including Mary. By selling Mary's portion, the Lincolns were able to buy their first home and move out of the rented cottage.

Portrait of Mary Lincoln's father, Robert S. Todd, painted by her niece, Katherine Helm, in the 1920s (based on an earlier portrait by an unknown Philadelphia artist, about 1836)

Robert Lincoln in 1861. His birth eighteen years earlier brought Robert Todd to Springfield to see his namesake grandson.

14. LINCOLN'S TEMPERANCE ADDRESS

ABRAHAM LINCOLN'S "TEMPERANCE ADDRESS," DELIVERED in the packed chapel of the Second Presbyterian Church, was preceded by a colorful street parade and enthusiastic communal singing in celebration of Washington's Birthday in February 1842. The Washingtonians—a national temperance association made up primarily of former drinkers—sponsored the event. Lincoln himself was a nondrinker. Nevertheless, he had generally stayed aloof from temperance societies, caricaturing their membership as predominantly *"Preachers, Lawyers, and hired agents"* who lacked *"approachability."* He criticized their tendency to address society's alcohol problem through legal coercion and *"too much denunciation."* The Washingtonians, however, he viewed

The Second Presbyterian Church (located on Fourth Street from 1840 to 1871) was still relatively new when Lincoln delivered his "Temperance Address" from its pulpit. Members of the congregation tended to have New England backgrounds and agitated for controversial social reforms such as temperance and abolition. Church discipline could be strict—one member was excommunicated for attending a public ball! The Church's Rev. Albert Hale, an abolitionist, was one of only three local ministers who supported Lincoln for president.

differently. He accepted their speaking invitation and became a member. Having been *"victims of intemperance"* themselves, Lincoln deemed them now to be the *"chief apostles"* of temperance. Their message of individual self-control directed at persuading drinkers to voluntarily abstain from alcohol appealed to Lincoln's sense of persuasive leadership. He rankled the self-righteous in attendance by declaring, *"such of us as have never fallen victims have been spared more by the absence of appetite than from any mental or moral superiority over those who have."*

LINCOLN WAS BORN INTO AN

"alcoholic republic." By the time he moved to Illinois in 1830, per capita consumption of hard liquor reached its historic high in the United States—over five gallons for every man, woman, and child in America. Given the extensive social damage created by so much drinking, it is not surprising that temperance became the most prevalent reform movement in pre–Civil War America. Springfield was typical in that during the period there arose more than a half-dozen temperance organizations. Temperance reform had an impact, but large segments of the population remained unaffected. At the time of his presidential inauguration Lincoln is reported to have jokingly dismissed assassination threats by remarking that he *"had often experienced a much greater fear in addressing a dozen Western men on the subject of temperance."*

In this Illinois temperance broadside, reformers compare a community that shuns alcohol with one that doesn't, asking parents, "[I]n which of these two towns would you train your children?"

15. GLOBE TAVERN

ABRAHAM AND MARY LINCOLN SPENT THEIR WEDDING NIGHT

at the Globe Tavern, and lived there for almost the first year of their marriage. It was not the fanciest hotel in Springfield, but Abraham considered it *"very well kept."* Their room—8 by 14 feet long—was the same one that Mary's sister Frances had occupied for three years as a young bride. Meals were shared with other boarders at a common dining table. The $8.00 monthly rent also included laundry service. Here their first child, Robert, was born. The situation was not ideal for a young mother and baby. Quarters were close. The mostly male guests could be noisy. And the tavern was a stage line office, so every

The Globe Tavern as it appeared in May 1865, at the time of Lincoln's funeral. The Lincolns lived here from November 1842 until the autumn of 1843. At that time the tavern consisted of two buildings joined as a "T," with the older portion extending out behind the newer addition (in which the Lincolns lived) which fronted Adams Street. Whig politicians tended to patronize the Globe, especially when the state legislature was in session. Proprietorship changed hands several times. Cyrus G. Saunders ran the establishment when the Lincolns moved in.

GLOBE HOTEL.

THE undersigned takes this method to inform the public in general, that he has taken possession of the Globe Hotel. in Springfield, Illinois, situated a few rods west of the State House, (formerly occupied by Col. G W. Spotswood) where he will at all times be happy to accommodate all who may give him a call.

He flatters himself by strict attention to business to merit a share of public patronage.

C. G. SAUNDERS.

—

Ye strangers who for enterprise may roam,
We here invite you to a friendly home.
Where always ready with an anxious care,
To serve our guests with choice substantial fare,
Pledg'd we stand to set a plenteous board,
With every wish the season can afford;
And when fatigue demands a peaceful rest,
We give you beds and bedding of the best.
N. B.   The Stabling, too, we confident commend,
And sober Ostlers willing to attend,
To all who sojourn through a Western course,
With tired oxen, jaded mule or horse.
February 18, 1840.   433 3m

A poem advertisement published in the local newspaper, the Sangamo Journal

time a coach arrived a bell would ring, calling stable boys to come care for the horses. Undoubtedly it was difficult to calm a fussy baby into slumber or to keep a sleeping baby from awaking. Guests reportedly complained about Robert's crying. This may have been a reason why the Lincolns moved and rented a nearby cottage in the fall of 1843. When Lincoln's friends David Davis and his wife lodged here the next year, Mrs. Davis complained that the proprietors scrimped on candles and used too much baking soda in their cakes, turning them *"quite yellow."*

IT WAS NOT UNCOMMON IN THE EARLY PART OF THE 19TH CENTURY

for newlyweds to start married life in a boardinghouse out of economic necessity, even though the evolving customs of polite society discouraged it. Social reformers feared that such circumstances prevented young wives from learning household duties, and that they would become idle and indolent, or even lose their virtue in the predominantly masculine environment. The daughter of a political enemy later claimed that her mother attended to Mary and her baby daily in the month after Robert was born, and that she, at six years of age, was permitted to tend Robert—on occasion dragging him through a hole in the tavern yard fence to lay him down in the tall prairie grass. How, she later wondered, could Mary have trusted *"a particularly small six year old with this charge?"*

16. FIRST PRESBYTERIAN CHURCH

ABRAHAM LINCOLN DIDN'T ATTEND CHURCH AS OFTEN AS HIS

wife, Mary. Perhaps comfort was a factor. A visiting minister once observed Lincoln's *"long legs stretched out in the middle of the isle to keep them from . . . being scrounged in the narrow space between the pews."* Lincoln rejected his Baptist upbringing and was reportedly a religious skeptic as a young man. The fatalistic outlook he retained throughout his life, however, reflected the Calvinistic influences of his youth. His closest friend, Joshua Speed,

The Lincolns rented a pew at the First Presbyterian Church beginning in 1852. Mary became a church member; Abraham didn't. Their youngest son, Tad, was baptized here at age two—apparently the only Lincoln child to receive baptism. In 1872 the First Presbyterian Church moved to its present location on Seventh Street near today's Lincoln Home visitors' center.

considered Lincoln a *"growing man in religion."* Lincoln read the King James Bible, knew it well, and loved its language which he used effectively and often. *"He was not a technical Christian,"* Mary once remarked. Still, she considered him a *"religious man always"* in morals and ethics. Lincoln's close associate, Judge David Davis, agreed that Lincoln *"had no faith in the Christian sense of that term."* But he also admitted, *"I don't know anything about Lincoln's religion—I don't think anybody knew."*

THE REV. JAMES SMITH WAS THE

resident pastor for much of the time the Lincolns attended the First Presbyterian Church. He was a Scotsman who as a young man doubted religion. He came to America at age 26 and converted to Christianity at a frontier revival, becoming a Presbyterian clergyman. His ministering to the Lincolns after their son Eddie died eventually resulted in Mary's joining his congregation. Smith based his faith on reason and logic rather than emotion and sentiment. His sophisticated 650-page book *The Christian's Defense* appealed to Lincoln's sense of rationality and may have influenced Lincoln's evolving religious sensibilities. Smith retired to his native Scotland after 1856. During the Civil War, Lincoln appointed him American Consul there. Mary and Tad stayed with Smith while visiting Europe after the war. He publicly supported Mary in her quarrels with Lincoln's biographer and former law partner, William Herndon.

The Rev. James Smith delivered the funeral sermon for the Lincolns' son Eddie.

Mary Lincoln joined the First Presbyterian Church after her son Eddie's death.

17. LINCOLN'S FUNERAL TRAIN

PEOPLE DESCENDED ON SPRINGFIELD FROM ALL DIRECTIONS

on the morning of May 3, 1865, to meet the train that brought Lincoln's body home. They began to gather early at the Chicago & Alton Railroad Depot. Thousands jammed the city's streets and rooftops by the time the train arrived at 9:00 A.M.—only one hour late after traveling for 13 days and 1,700 miles across the country. Silence prevailed as an honor guard transferred the coffin to a special hearse loaned by the mayor of St. Louis. Soldiers lined both sides of Jefferson Street, forming a corridor of honor for the fallen commander in chief, whose body was borne down the street to lie in state in the Old State Capitol for one last public viewing.

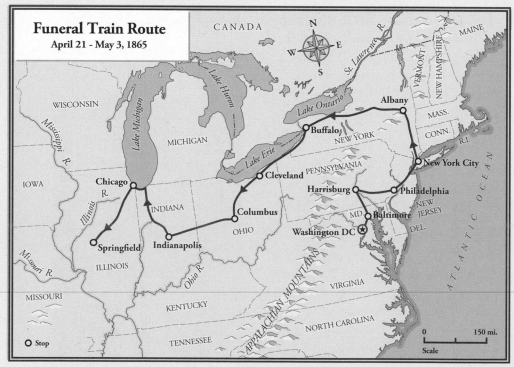

Funeral Train Route
April 21 - May 3, 1865

The Lincoln funeral train stopped in ten different cities along the route for memorial services and public viewings. Historians estimate that almost one in four Americans saw either Lincoln's coffin or the nine-car funeral train that carried it. Never before had there been an event that emotionally tied Americans together in a single shared national experience on such a vast scale.

RAILROADS FASCINATED WILLIE LINCOLN. THIS WAS NATURAL, GIVEN

that his childhood in the 1850s corresponded with an explosive growth in railroads that generated excitement similar to what children of the 1960s experienced during the space race to the moon. Toy makers recognized the interest. Soon boys across the country, including Willie, were playing with train sets. Willie memorized railroad timetables and conducted imaginary train trips from New York to Chicago that revealed a special aptitude for mathematics—a trait he shared with his father. Like his son, Lincoln was also intrigued by trains. He supported them as a state legislator. He argued many railroad company court cases (both for and against). He became so good that the Illinois Central Railroad placed him on permanent retainer so he couldn't represent opponents. As president he promoted building the first transcontinental railroad.

Mourners gathering at the Chicago & Alton Railroad Depot awaiting the arrival of Lincoln's funeral train. During the 1850s Lincoln had boarded many trains at this depot. Here he introduced former president Millard Fillmore to Springfield citizens when Fillmore's train briefly stopped in 1854. Here Lincoln met with William H. Seward (a man he defeated for the Republican nomination and who would become his secretary of state) when Seward's train stopped briefly during the 1860 presidential campaign. However, when the Prince of Wales (England's future king Edward VII) stopped here for a few minutes in September 1860 during an Illinois bird-hunting tour, presidential-candidate Lincoln missed meeting him.

The mayor of St. Louis loaned this hearse for use in the Springfield funeral.

Willie Lincoln loved trains.

William Butler's red brick boardinghouse—where bachelor Lincoln ate meals and took his laundry—once stood in the vicinity of the train tracks on the southwest corner of Madison and Third Streets. Butler didn't charge Lincoln for board. He even bought him clothes and paid some of his debts. Lincoln reportedly saved the life of Butler's youngest son by tearing off the toddler's scalding clothes when the child pulled a pot of boiling coffee down onto himself.

"MR. LINCOLN DID PROPOSE MARRIAGE TO ME," SARAH RICKARD

confirmed when asked about the subject in her later years. Sarah developed a close friendship with Lincoln as she assisted her sister Elizabeth (Mrs. William Butler) in managing the boardinghouse where Lincoln took his meals. Though fifteen years separated Lincoln and Sarah, he sometimes escorted her to social events. One evening in 1840 when they were alone in the parlor, Lincoln declared, *"Now Sarah, you know your Bible well enough to know that Sarah was Abraham's wife."* Surprised and embarrassed, Sarah quickly left the room. *"I always liked him as a friend but . . . his peculiar manner and his general deportment . . . [did not] fascinate a young girl just entering the society world,"* she explained, admitting later, *"If I'd known that he would have been President I would have paid more attention to him."* Instead, Sarah married Richard F. Barret, whom Lincoln appointed to a federal land office job during the Civil War. The Barrets eventually moved to Kansas City where both are buried in the Elmwood Cemetery.

WHEN WILLIAM BUTLER FIRST

met Abraham Lincoln paddling a canoe on the Sangamon River in 1831, he considered him *"as ruff a specimen of humanity as could be found."* In the following years Butler observed firsthand important episodes in Lincoln's career—service in the Black Hawk War, the legislative battle in Vandalia to move the state capital to Springfield, Lincoln's aborted saber duel with James Shields, his failed Senate campaigns, and the 1860 Republican Convention in Chicago where Butler helped to nominate the once *"ruff specimen"* for president. Not all was smooth in their relationship, however. A grudge based on Congressman Lincoln's refusal to procure him a federal job apparently caused Butler to secretly oppose Lincoln's first bid for the U.S. Senate in 1855. Nevertheless, in 1860 Butler rode Lincoln's presidential electoral coattails to election as Illinois state treasurer.

Sarah Rickard in her later years, after her marriage to Richard F. Barret

WILLIAM BUTLER.

William Butler, a supporter who sometimes considered Lincoln ungrateful

19. CHENERY HOUSE

ABRAHAM LINCOLN SPENT HIS LAST NIGHT IN SPRINGFIELD IN

the Chenery House. Three days before leaving for Washington, Lincoln moved his family into rooms on the second floor facing Fourth Street. With their furniture sold and their house rented out, they made their final preparations for moving while boarding here. Eleven-year-old Willie Lincoln persisted in blowing out the fancy gaslight jets in their hotel room. When reprimanded, the boy told his father that he had always been allowed to blow out the oil lamps at home. On the morning of February 11, 1861, Lincoln roped up the family's trunks with his own hands. Taking some hotel cards, he wrote on the back: "A. Lincoln, White House, Washington, D.C.," and tacked one on each trunk. He left for the train station riding in the hotel's horse-drawn omnibus,

When a Republican legislator from out of town asked Lincoln for help in finding a room, Lincoln replied, "I suppose the 'Chenery House' is likely to be the Republican Head Quarters. . . . [T]he best that can be done there is . . . $21 per week, with fire and light, for two persons. I do not believe you can do better, at any of the Hotels."

passing at the southeast end of the block the old store where 24 years earlier he had spent his *first* night as a resident of Springfield.

THE CHENERY HOUSE BECAME ONE

of Springfield's premier hotels in 1855 after John W. Chenery, former manager of the American House, remodeled the old City Hotel that once stood here. A committee of Lincoln's wealthy Springfield friends paid the hotel bill for important national politicians when they came to meet with Lincoln during and after the 1860 presidential campaign. Lincoln's secretary, John Nicolay (whose office was directly across Fourth Street to the west), sadly remarked that the hotel became so crowded that he had to *"scramble"* for dinner. Gen. Ulysses S. Grant's first Civil War headquarters were here. Illinois' wartime governor, Richard Yates, reviewed and addressed departing troops from the balcony over the hotel's main entrance, while Mrs. Chenery sang renditions of the "Star Spangled Banner." Later, the first floor of the hotel became a soldier's hospital.

Illinois governor Richard Yates, circa 1860s

Gen. Ulysses S. Grant stayed at the Chenery House while training troops in Springfield during the earliest days of the Civil War.

20. BRUNSWICK'S BILLIARD HALL

LINCOLN WAS KNOWN TO PLAY BILLIARDS. HE EVIDENTLY

played it with lawyers and townsfolk in various halls and taverns along the judicial circuit. While awaiting news of his presidential nomination he went to an *"excellent and neat beer saloon"* to play but found the tables occupied. Watching Lincoln play billiards was apparently entertaining; his unorthodox form and style was amusingly *"awkard."* Though not of championship caliber, he was reportedly no worse than the average amateur. Nevertheless, as president he once demonstrated a trick shot to a bemused official. With the aid of a pen, hat, and inkstands spread atop a common table, he showed how a skillful player could *"strike a ball on one side and hit a ball on the opposite side of the hat, without touching the hat."*

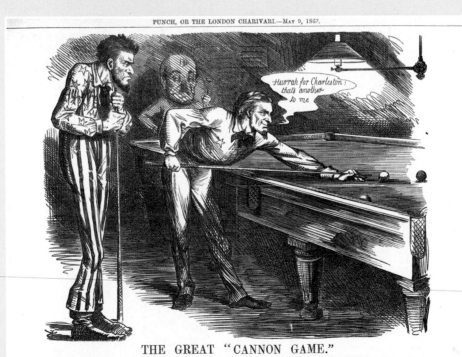

THE GREAT "CANNON GAME."

ABE LINCOLN (ASIDE). "DARN'D IF HE AIN'T SCORED AG'IN!—WISH I COULD MAKE A FEW *WINNING* HAZARDS FOR A CHANGE."

Billiards started as an elite game for high society. By Lincoln's time it had spread to common taverns and saloons and was associated with drinking and gambling. Lincoln's wartime critics caricatured him as a shiftless billiards player, likening the presidential mansion to "an enlarged edition of an Illinois bar room."

An advertisement from the 1863 Springfield City Directory

IN 1860 EMANUEL BRUNSWICK OPENED A BILLIARD HALL IN THE

second floor of the building just east of the Chenery House on Washington Street. It contained elegant Brunswick tables and was touted as the largest and best hall in Illinois outside Chicago. A local paper reported, *"There is no place so worthy the attention of strangers and citizens who wish to see boys enjoying themselves, and where no gambling is allowed."* The popularity of billiards by the 1860s reflected a rise in leisure activities that resulted from the growth of cities and the relative easing of living conditions. Also, technical innovations had improved the game—leather-tipped cues replaced tipless tapered poles of ash or maple; rubberized side cushions replaced cloth sleeves stuffed with cotton, sawdust, feathers, or strips of felt; slate table beds replaced warp-prone wood. The Billiard Hall's eloquently crafted Brunswick tables reflected both technical improvements and societal change.

Hoffman's Row was considered "a striking and handsome improvement" over other buildings in early Springfield. It consisted of six two-storied contiguous brick sections that ran north up Fifth Street to the middle of the block. A second-floor room in the fifth section was the law office of Stuart and Lincoln. Furnishings were a small lounge, a chair, a buffalo robe, a wooden bench, bookcase, and table "which answered for a desk."

BEFORE HE MOVED TO SPRINGFIELD ABRAHAM LINCOLN CAME

to the law office of John Todd Stuart to borrow law books. Henry E. Dummer—Stuart's partner at the time—recalled that the *"uncouth looking"* Lincoln said little and seemed timid. Yet when he did talk he was both strong and acute. *"He surprised us more and more at every visit,"* Dummer remembered. In 1837 Lincoln joined Stuart as the junior in a law partnership that lasted four years. At the time, Sangamon County rented the room directly beneath the partners' law office as a courtroom. A trapdoor between the ceiling and floor connected the rooms. This permitted Lincoln to *"overhear"* a lot. During the fall 1839 political season, disgruntled Democrats threatened Lincoln's friend Edward Baker with bodily harm during a speech Baker was delivering in the courtroom. Hearing the commotion, the 30-year-old Lincoln made a sudden, dramatic entrance through the trap-door into the crowd. He threatened to *"pitch in"* if anyone attacked Baker. No one challenged Lincoln. Baker finished his speech unmolested.

IN LINCOLN'S WORLD THERE WERE

few schools in which to study law and politics. For most young men, a mentor was indispensable. Lincoln's first was John Todd Stuart—an educated Kentucky aristocrat who was two years Lincoln's senior (and a first cousin to Mary Todd, the future Mrs. Lincoln). Stuart met Lincoln as a militia officer during the Black Hawk War and worked with him as a state legislator in Vandalia. Impressed by Lincoln's demeanor and intelligence, he encouraged Lincoln to study law. He also guided Lincoln into the circles of political leadership. In the 1850s they became politically estranged when Stuart refused to join the antislavery Republican Party after the demise of the Whig party. During the Civil War Stuart won election to Congress as a Democrat, defeating one of Lincoln's protégés in an embarrassing defeat for the president.

John Todd Stuart, Lincoln's early mentor and first law partner

STUART & LINCOLN,
ATTORNEYS and Counsellors at Law, will practice, conjointly, in the Courts of this Judicial Circuit.— Office No. 4 Hoffman's Row, up stairs.
Springfield, april 12, 1837.   4

April 1837 advertisement in Springfield's newspaper the Sangamo Journal

22. JOSHUA SPEED'S STORE

Joshua F. Speed was 22 years old and part-owner of the store that stood here in 1837. Speed was the son of an affluent Kentucky plantation owner and had more formal education than Lincoln. The two roommates shared anxieties about women and consoled each other in matters of courtship and marriage. Their deep friendship lasted throughout Lincoln's life.

THERE WAS A HOUSING

shortage in Springfield when 28-year-old Abraham Lincoln—riding a borrowed horse—moved from New Salem in April 1837. Builders couldn't keep up with the demand for housing in the newly designated state capital. One of Lincoln's first stops was at the general store located here. An old New Salem friend, Abner Y. Ellis, was part-owner. But Ellis was not in when Lincoln called. Instead, he was greeted by another partner, Joshua Speed. Lincoln needed furnishings for a bed but admitted he couldn't afford them. *"I looked up at him,"* Speed recalled, *"and thought . . . I never saw so gloomy and melancholy a face."* Speed offered to share his second-floor room and large double bed with Lincoln. Without saying a word, Lincoln threw his saddlebags over his arm, trudged upstairs, and dropped them on the floor. Coming down again *"with a face beaming with pleasure and smiles,"* Lincoln declared: *"Well Speed, I'm moved."*

MEN OUTNUMBERED WOMEN ALMOST TWO TO ONE WHEN LINCOLN

arrived in Springfield. Like Lincoln, many men were unmarried and in their twenties. Thrown together in rooming houses sharing beds and close quarters, many took their meals in boardinghouses that were often in different buildings. A young-male subculture arose, where men fraternized in the evenings. Drinking and card playing was prevalent. But so too were attempts at cultivating middle-class respectability. Men discussed poetry and philosophy, and shared literary compositions. Joshua Speed later remembered that *"on every winter's night at my store by a big wood fire . . . eight or ten choice spirits assembled"* to enjoy each other's company and wit. One December night they *"got to talking politics"* and tempers flared. Stephen Douglas suddenly declared, *"Gentlemen, this is no place to talk politics!"* Good will returned as they resumed their usual banter, including doses of Lincoln's infectious humor.

Among the bachelors enjoying this game of cards was James H. Matheny (left), who served as best man at Lincoln's wedding.

23. LINCOLN'S LAST LAW OFFICE

THE PRESENT LAW OFFICE OF ABRAHAM LINCOLN, THE PRESIDENT ELECT, IN FIFTH STREET, WEST SIDE OF THE PUBLIC SQUARE, SPRINGFIELD, ILL.—FROM A SKETCH BY OUR SPECIAL ARTIST.

Lincoln and Herndon rented law offices at several locations over the years. Their last was a rear room on the second floor in a building that stood on Fifth Street. Leslie's Weekly published this drawing of the office interior soon after the 1860 presidential campaign. It contradicts contemporary descriptions of a "dingy" and "untidy" office. Its windows overlooked back alleys and tar-covered roofs. In hot weather the room sometimes had a caustic resin smell. "A law office is a dry place for incidents of a pleasing kind," Herndon observed.

ABRAHAM LINCOLN'S THIRD AND FINAL LAW PARTNER WAS

William H. Herndon. He was nine years Lincoln's junior. They practiced together from 1844 to 1861. Arriving at work Lincoln would tease, "*Billy*— how is your *bones* philosophy this morning?" Working in the shadow of his celebrated senior partner, Herndon did much of the legal research for their cases and managed the office during Lincoln's frequent absences. After Lincoln died, Herndon hoped to write the definitive biography of his famous friend. He collected reminiscences from all sorts of people. Herndon's interview notes, correspondence, and Lincoln biography are important sources regarding the pre-presidential Lincoln. Mary Lincoln and others were greatly offended at some of Herndon's allegations—among them, that Lincoln was a religious skeptic and that his only true love was New Salem's Ann Rutledge. Mary called Herndon a "*hopeless inebriate*" and a "*dirty dog.*" Herndon called

Mary *"the female wildcat of the age."* Herndon battled alcoholism and died in relative poverty in 1891.

HIS LAW OFFICE WAS ONE OF THE

last places Lincoln visited before he left Springfield to become president. In the late afternoon of February 10, 1861—his last full day in Springfield—Lincoln came here to discuss unfinished legal business and to reminisce with his partner of over sixteen years, William Herndon. According to Herndon, Lincoln asked that he leave their doorway shingle in place—*"Let it hang there undisturbed,"* he instructed—until his work in Washington was done and he could return to resume his law practice with Herndon once again. One last time the two men stepped down the familiar dark, narrow stairwell, then walked together into the fading afternoon light, the senior partner never to cross the office threshold again.

The windows in Lincoln's last law office overlooked back alleys and tar-covered rooftops. The building no longer exists.

The earliest-known picture of William H. Herndon, circa 1870

The Tinsley Building on the southwest corner of Sixth and Adams streets is the only Springfield building that still exists where Lincoln had law offices. Today it is administered by the Illinois Historic Preservation Agency as the Lincoln-Herndon Law Offices State Historic Site.

24. SIMEON FRANCIS HOME

Simeon Francis lived in a house on the corner where the Abraham Lincoln Presidential Library stands today. No picture of the house is known to exist. Tradition holds that Lincoln, as a young politician from New Salem, was so affected by Francis's editorials that he walked the twenty miles to Springfield for the sole purpose of meeting the editor.

PARTISAN EDITORS WERE KEY players in the rough-and-tumble political world of pre–Civil War America. Successful politicians needed a strong editorial ally. Simeon Francis played that role for Illinois' Whig politicians, including Abraham Lincoln. As editor of Springfield's *Illinois State Journal* from 1831 to 1855, Francis was a power in state politics. He was *"warmly attached to Lincoln . . . and entertained great admiration for Lincoln's brains and noble qualities."* One of Lincoln's letters regarding Francis reveals the rowdy nature of Illinois politics: *"Yesterday [Stephen] Douglas, having chosen to consider himself insulted by something in the 'Journal,' undertook to cane Francis in the street. Francis caught him by the hair and jammed him back against a market-cart, where the matter ended by Francis being pulled away from him. The whole affair was so ludicrous that Francis and everybody else (Douglas excepted) have been laughing about it ever since."* Francis moved to Oregon the year before Lincoln was elected president. Lincoln appointed him to be an army paymaster after the war started.

ABRAHAM AND MARY HELD SECRET TRYSTS IN THE PARLOR OF THE

Francis home after they resumed their courtship in the autumn of 1842. For reasons that are still subject to speculation, the two had abruptly broken their marriage engagement on New Year's Day in 1841. Simeon's wife, Eliza Francis, was fond of Lincoln. Also, she shared Mary's intense interest in politics—a trait that set them apart from most of their female peers. Sensing their mutual unhappiness—and perhaps hoping to facilitate an advantageous political union—Eliza decided to play romantic and political matchmaker. She contrived to bring the couple together in her home for a secret reconciliation. It worked. To avoid the disapproving eyes of Mary's family, the two continued meeting privately at the Francis home until their marriage on November 4, 1842.

Artifacts found during archeological digs conducted at the Francis house site before construction began on the Abraham Lincoln Presidential Library

25. THE "BALL ALLEY"

LINCOLN LOVED THE GAME OF "FIVES." THE GAME WAS AN
early form of handball brought to America by Irish immigrants. "Fives"
represented the five fingers used in striking a ball against a wall. Opposing
players had to return the ball against the wall in one hop. Several men usually
played at once. Lincoln-era handball courts were generally larger than modern
versions; balls were harder and traveled faster. One Springfield player recalled
that Lincoln's *"suppleness, leaps and strides to strike the ball were comical in
the extreme."* He must have been effective, however, for alley-keeper William
Donnelly recalled that Lincoln was *"one of the most active and skillful players,
his success being due to his agility and large hands, enabling him to catch the ball
almost every time."* An English enthusiast declared, *"[Fives] is the finest experience for the body, and the best relaxation for the mind."* Lincoln is reported to
have simply said, *"This game makes my shoulders feel well."*

*During the anxious days of the 1860 Republican Convention in Chicago, Lincoln reportedly
played "Fives" (handball) against the wall in the "Ball Alley" south of the Illinois State
Journal Building (site now occupied by the southern portion of the Abraham Lincoln
Presidential Library). He was apparently inside the Journal office when he received news of
his presidential nomination.*

This pro-Lincoln political cartoon from September 1860 caricatures presidential candidates as baseball club members. For a bat, Lincoln wields one of his campaign symbols—a split-rail.

SPRINGFIELD'S BALL ALLEY WAS A POPULAR PLACE FOR MEN TO

congregate for exercise and amusement. Young professional men formed a ball club that met there regularly. The alley was leveled, smoothed, and maintained by an attendant. Fees were charged for admittance. Younger men played an early version of football for free on the prairie south of the city. Springfield also had a baseball club. Though apparently not a club member, Lincoln was reportedly a good player. A participant remembered he *"could catch a ball; he would strip and go at it—do it well."* Foot racing was popular (Lincoln was reportedly a fast runner). So was *"hopping."* Lincoln *"hopped well,"* a friend recalled. *"In three hops he would go 40.2 on a dead level."*

26. SPRINGFIELD MARINE & FIRE INSURANCE COMPANY

Robert Irwin was prominent in local business affairs and was Lincoln's friend and political ally. He was one of the founders of the Springfield Marine & Fire Insurance Company, serving as cashier and bookkeeper. When Lincoln left to become president he made Irwin his financial agent in Springfield. Irwin died a month before his friend was assassinated.

ABRAHAM LINCOLN OPENED A bank account here in 1853. When he left to become president he had assets worth about $15,000—a tidy sum, but far less than the fortunes amassed by many of his colleagues. He largely avoided the rampant land speculation of his time, thinking he had *"no capacity whatever"* for it. *"His love of wealth was very weak,"* an associate remarked. *"All the use Mr. Lincoln had for wealth was to enable him to appear respectable."* His law partner Herndon, however, groused that while Lincoln *"had no avarice of the GET"* he did have *"avarice of the KEEP,"* and that *"he was not generous in his money matters."* Still, Lincoln was apparently sincere in his belief that *"wealth is simply a superfluity of what we don't need."* Perhaps this personal indifference toward wealth explains why Lincoln, a skilled attorney in matters of other people's money, died without having drafted a last will and testament of his own!

MANY PEOPLE DIDN'T TRUST BANKS

in Lincoln's time. In the 1830s President Andrew Jackson repeatedly attacked the national bank as a corrupt institution. Then an economic depression caused many banks to fail, including the Illinois State Bank in 1842. Money was scarce; financial hardship was widespread. The 1847 Illinois Constitution reflected public distrust by making it almost impossible to charter new banks. But commercial growth and economic recovery stalled without adequate banking services. Finally the Illinois legislature circumvented constitutional restrictions by granting banking powers to insurance companies. When chartered in 1851 the Springfield Marine & Fire Insurance Company opened on the east side of the public square in a Grecian-columned building that had formerly housed the state bank. It provided essential banking services to the community into the 20th century. It never did exercise its chartered powers as an insurance company.

Lincoln did his banking in this classical-style building, home of the Springfield Marine & Fire Insurance Company. Previously it had housed the Illinois State Bank before the state legislature terminated it.

The bank (columned building on the right) as seen from the Old State Capitol cupola. The columned building to the left of it became the Sangamon County Courthouse in 1846. Lincoln tried state circuit court cases there.

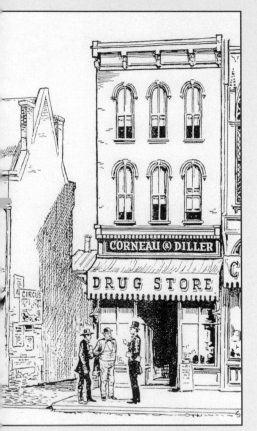

In 1849 partners Roland W. Diller and Charles S. Corneau opened their store on the east side of the public square. With its big stove and circle of chairs amid cluttered shelves of drugs, pills, patent medicines, and other articles, it became a favorite place for men—including Abraham Lincoln—to congregate and discuss politics and social happenings, and to swap stories.

APOTHECARIES IN THE MID-19TH

century carried a surprising variety of drugs and remedies—potassium iodide for rheumatism and syphilis, sulphate of quinine for tooth powder, opium elixir for toothache, and camphor for an aphrodisiac. "Cure-all" patent medicines were popular. "Dr. Hoofland's Balsamic Cordial" was touted for dysentery and colic. "Wright's Indian Vegetable Pills" cured *"headaches, hysterics, weak nerves, low spirits, female complaints, and stomach and lung disorders."* Sarsaparilla was prescribed for *"ringworms, lumbago, pains of the bones and joints, neuralgia, nervous debility, and pale complexion."* "Brown Mixture," named for its color, was Corneau & Diller's own remedy for colds and coughs. Because Springfield's first soda fountain was installed here, Robert Lincoln later recalled that he and his friends considered Corneau & Diller *"a good place to go."*

LEDGER RECORDS OF THE LINCOLNS' STORE ACCOUNT SHOW THAT

Mary Lincoln purchased toiletries such as bear's oil, ox marrow, "French Chalk" for her complexion, a patent hairdressing called "Zylobalsam," and "Mrs. Allen's Restorative." She made cosmetic paste out of Castile soap and Indian meal. Because daily bathing was not yet customary, the Lincolns—like most other people—bought cologne by the quart! For the children, Mary purchased "Pennyroyal" to prevent flea and mosquito bites, "Hive Syrup" for coughs and croup, "Wistar's Balsam of Wild Cherry" for asthma and bronchitis, and sweet oil for chest rubs. It seems the Lincoln children often suffered respiratory ailments. Three of them eventually died prematurely from fevers or lung disease.

C. S. CORNEAU.   R. W. DILLER

CORNEAU & DILLER.
WHOLESALE AND RETAIL DRUGGISTS
East Side of the Public Square.
SPRINGFIELD, ILLINOIS.

WOULD respectfully return grateful thanks for the liberal patronage bestowed upon them during the past year and solicit a continuance of the same.

We have now on hand a well selected stock of drugs, medicines, and chemicals, paints, oils, varnish and dye-stuffs, window glass, putty and glassware, perfumery, fine soaps and tooth brushes, paint brushes, spices, snuff and fine chewing tobacco.

Pure wine and brandies for medicinal purposes.

☞ Physician's prescriptions will receive particular attention at all hours of the day and night.

☞ Customers and physicians will always find at this establishment fresh and unadulterated medicines which have been selected with great personal care for this market. All purchasers are invited to examine the stock, as they will find it equal to any other in the state.

Orders from the country promptly filled and satisfaction guaranteed, with regard both to price and quality.

feb 24 '52—yl   CORNEAU & DILLER.

DIARRHŒA AND CHOLERA MIXTURE.
As recommended by the Board of Health.

THE above medicine was recommended by the Board of Health in 1849 and '50, as one of the greatest preventatives of cholera and cure of diarrhœa then known, and further use and experience has shown that it may be used with complete success in the premonitory symptoms. Every family should have a bottle of it in their house so they can lay their hands on it in a moment's warning.

☞ Price 25 cents per bottle. To be had at all times of CORNEAU & DILLER,

June 2.   east side public square.

Roland W. Diller

This October 1854 advertisement reveals the drug store sold "pure wine and brandies," but only "for medicinal purposes."

28. COOK'S HALL

POLITICAL AND RELIGIOUS EVENTS WERE IMPORTANT PUBLIC

entertainments in Lincoln's day—but people also enjoyed fairs, militia drills, parades, circuses, dances, dinner parties, concerts, plays, and lectures. Initially such events were held outdoors. But as villages became more citified, residents built spacious indoor meeting places. Cook's Hall was one of several public halls that graced the capital city at various times from the mid-1830s to the Civil War. The Hall opened with a vocal recital in December 1858. Over the next two years visiting theatrical troupes, military drill teams, musical ensembles, magicians, scientists, authors, poets, artists, world travelers, and other lecturers appeared here—Ralph Waldo Emerson, Horace Greeley, Henry Ward Beecher, and Theodore Parker among them. The notorious Lola Montez—dancer, actress, and former mistress of the King of Bavaria—set disapproving tongues wagging with her lecture "Fashion" to a packed hall in the spring of 1860.

When it opened in 1858, Cook's Hall (at right) became the largest of Springfield's public halls. Its gaslit auditorium and gallery were the grandest in the region. A wealthy soap and candle manufacturer, John Cook, built the hall following a devastating fire that burned down a large portion of the block. Cook proudly christened his new building "Illiopolitan Hall." Townspeople preferred the less grandiose title of "Cook's Hall." It was here in April 1860—in the midst of presidential politics—that Abraham Lincoln delivered his scientific lecture, "Discoveries and Inventions," for the final time.

JOHN C. HEENAN REPORTEDLY

visited presidential candidate Abraham Lincoln in October 1860. Republican newspapers assured readers that Heenan was a *"warm admirer"* of Lincoln. Democratic newspapers countered that only the *"lower classes"* followed boxing. Heenan put on an exhibition match here the following December to a sold-out house. Boxing was a bare-knuckled sport in those days, and both Heenan and his opponent left for St. Louis after the fight to recuperate from their injuries. We don't know if Lincoln or his sons attended. As a former wrestler Lincoln may have wished to; Mary would probably have considered it beneath the dignity of the president-elect.

American boxing heavyweight champion John C. Heenan

Newspaper broadside advertising John C. Heenan's reception

29. THE AMERICAN HOUSE

Social galas and political functions were common at the American House, which is the building to the right of the state capitol in this picture.

A newspaper publicized Springfield's newest hotel under the direction of J. Clifton, a former Bostonian.

FOR MANY YEARS THE GRANDEST

hotel in Lincoln's Springfield was the American House. When it opened in November 1838, an Ohio editor extolled the *"Turkish splendor"* of its interior, stating that the carpeting, papering, and furniture *"weary the eye with magnificence."* On winter evenings when Springfield was full of visitors attending the state legislature, the hotel hosted popular Cotillion parties. A December 1840 guest recorded in her diary a scene from the "Ladies' Parlor" during a party:

A number of the ladies carried bundles in their arms and were accompanied by maids. The bundles, which were a mystery to me, were deposited on the bed, where the mystery soon developed, for the bundles began to kick and squeal, as hungry babies will. The mothers, after performing their maternal duties, wrapped the infants up again and left them with many charges to nursemaids not to mix them up. The ladies were handsomely dressed, but not in the latest style. They wore handsome gowns of silk and satin, made with low necks and short sleeves.

TRADITION HOLDS THAT LINCOLN

escorted former president Martin Van Buren to the American House in June 1842. Van Buren was a Democrat. Lincoln was a Whig. But Lincoln's renown for humor purportedly earned him an invitation to meet with Van Buren at the nearby village of Rochester. For one enjoyable evening, the *future president* is said to have entertained the *former president* with his wit and stories. The next day local citizens escorted Van Buren into the city. Here at the American House the former president received crowds of callers and enjoyed a party in his honor. Van Buren had been portrayed as something of a "dandy" by political opponents. Many in Springfield were surprised to find him *"an open, frank, plainly dressed man."*

A BEAUTIFUL GOBLET OF WHITE·HOUSE CHAMPAGNE

Lampoon of former U.S. president Martin Van Buren, who stayed at the American House in 1842. Springfield voters never gave him a majority in any of the three elections in which he ran for president, but most found him congenial on a personal level.

30. WILLIAM FLORVILLE'S BARBER SHOP

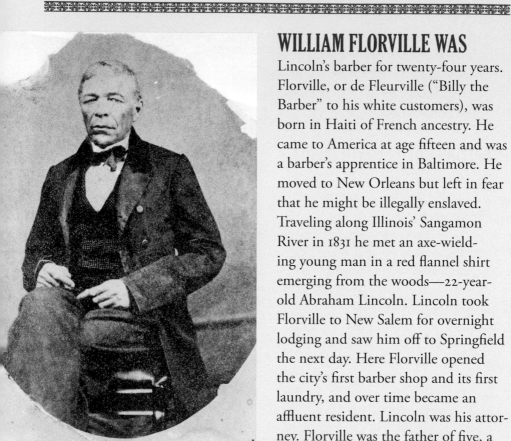

During most of the 1850s William Florville's barber shop was on the north side of Adams Street. Lincoln enjoyed loitering about the shop, sometimes forgetfully leaving law books there for days.

WILLIAM FLORVILLE WAS

Lincoln's barber for twenty-four years. Florville, or de Fleurville ("Billy the Barber" to his white customers), was born in Haiti of French ancestry. He came to America at age fifteen and was a barber's apprentice in Baltimore. He moved to New Orleans but left in fear that he might be illegally enslaved. Traveling along Illinois' Sangamon River in 1831 he met an axe-wielding young man in a red flannel shirt emerging from the woods—22-year-old Abraham Lincoln. Lincoln took Florville to New Salem for overnight lodging and saw him off to Springfield the next day. Here Florville opened the city's first barber shop and its first laundry, and over time became an affluent resident. Lincoln was his attorney. Florville was the father of five, a devoted Catholic, a supporter of local charities, and a popular musician. He was invited to join Springfield's dignitaries at the front of Lincoln's funeral procession. He chose instead to march at the rear where Springfield's African American delegation was assigned.

BARBERING WAS CLOSELY IDENTIFIED WITH AFRICAN AMERICANS IN

Lincoln's era. In 1850 Springfield had no white barbers, yet almost a quarter of the men who headed the city's twenty-seven independent black families were barbers. African Americans lived in small clusters throughout the city. More than twenty lived within three blocks of Lincoln's home. Laws and customs severely limited their economic and social opportunities. Most were employed as domestic servants or in trades of a servile nature. Barbering required little capital; success depended on pleasing a white clientele. The 1850s were difficult years for Springfield's black community. Hardening racial attitudes and intimidation caused many to leave. Also, increasing numbers of European immigrants competed with African Americans for menial jobs. By 1860 there were three white barbers in town—all German immigrants.

WM. FLORVILLE,
BARBER & HAIR-DRESSER.

BILLY will always be found on the spot,
With razors keen and water smoking hot;
He'll clip and dress your hair, and shave with ease
And leave no effort slack his friends to please.
His shop is north-west of the public square,
Just below the office of the Mayor;
Strangers or friends may always find him there,
Ready to shave them well or cut their hair.
On Sunday, until 9 o'clock he'll shave,
And then to church he'll go, his soul to save.
To his old customers, for favors past,
His gratitude, indeed, will ever last;
He hopes by attention and efforts rare,
A part of public patronage to share.

Florville often composed witty newspaper advertisements.

31. LINCOLN-ERA FIRE COMPANIES

Newspaper etching of city fire

LINCOLN'S SPRINGFIELD WAS VULNERABLE TO FIRE. CROWDED

wood-frame buildings; open flames in stoves, fireplaces, candles, and primitive gas lighting; ineffective alarms; impassable mud streets; and inadequate water supplies—all combined to make fires potentially devastating. Springfield had its share of fires. In 1855 a portion of the block west of the statehouse burned down, prompting citizens to become more serious about fire threats. Still, it took two more years to collect subscriptions to buy a "modern" pump carriage and organize an official fire company—the Pioneers. More companies soon followed. Then in February 1858 flames broke out on the square's east side; the fire quickly spread along Sixth Street, consuming all the shops in its path. Rounding the southwest corner on Adams Street, it destroyed more buildings, including Florville's barber shop. Firemen saved as much property as they could by dragging it into the street. Lincoln reportedly helped carry the iron stove out of Diller's burning drug store.

FIRE COMPANIES WERE IMPORTANT

social institutions in Lincoln's world. Much like volunteer militiamen, volunteer firemen enjoyed parading in handsome uniforms at community events and relished the parties, dances, and banquets sponsored by their companies. Companies would challenge each other in competitions to demonstrate their fire-fighting prowess. In 1858 a Jacksonville company came to Springfield for Fourth of July festivities. But play could be as dangerous as the real thing. During the competition a member of the Springfield company was severely injured by a bursting leather fire hose. In a banquet that day, Abraham Lincoln—an honored guest—offered the following toast to the hometown volunteers: *"The Pioneer Fire Company—May they extinguish all the bad flames, but keep the flame of patriotism ever burning brightly in the hearts of the ladies."*

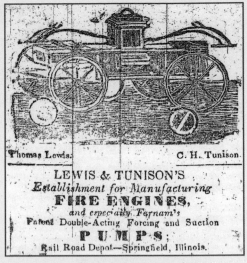

LEWIS & TUNISON'S
Establishment for Manufacturing
FIRE ENGINES,
and especially Farnam's
Patent Double-Acting Forcing and Suction
PUMPS;
Rail Road Depot—Springfield, Illinois.

Thomas Lewis. *C. H. Tunison.*

There were no fire hydrants in Lincoln's Springfield. Volunteers manned a hose carriage and hand-pumped water from several large public cisterns. When they were empty, firemen trampled over fences and gardens to reach private wells. As a homeowner Lincoln would have been expected to keep two leather buckets handy for an emergency bucket brigade.

FIREMANS' BALL
OF THE
SANGAMO FIRE COMPANY, NO. 2,
AT MYERS' CONCERT HALL,
On Monday, May 28th, 1860.
may 24d4t*

Firemans' Ball newspaper notice

Firemen used speaking trumpets to communicate over the din at fire scenes.

32. THE LYCEUM

LYCEUMS WERE COMMUNITY ASSOCIATIONS THAT SPONSORED lectures, debates, and discussions. Protestant missionaries and educators from the East brought the concept to frontier Illinois. Promoters hoped their lyceums would disseminate knowledge and encourage civic responsibility. Townspeople hoped attendance would help them climb the ladder of middle-class respectability. Aspiring local leaders used them as forums for honing their oratorical and analytic skills. In Lincoln's day there were over 3,000 lyceums nationwide. Springfield had two lyceums—the Sangamon County Lyceum, founded in 1833, followed a few years later by the Young Men's Lyceum. Meetings were usually on Saturday nights. Prominent local men—and those who hoped to be prominent—were invited as speakers. Topics included science,

From 1838 to 1840, the Young Men's Lyceum met in the Baptist Church, on the southwest corner of Seventh and Adams Streets. It was here that Lincoln delivered his famous "Lyceum Speech" on January 27, 1838. The church did not have the tall "battlement" tower at the time. It was added twenty-one years later—the year before Lincoln was elected president. The tower housed a 2,300-pound bell. It rang at Lincoln's election—and at his funeral.

culture, health, history, and politics. Participants discussed such questions as whether to abolish the death penalty, whether newspapers could be trusted, and whether married people were happier than single people. Since women also attended, lyceums had a social and recreational function, as well. At the lyceum, young men like Abraham Lincoln could simultaneously pursue their professional and social advancement.

A FEW WEEKS BEFORE HIS 29TH BIRTHDAY, ABRAHAM LINCOLN

addressed the Young Men's Lyceum. He responded to the question *"Do the signs of the present times indicate the downfall of this Government?"* His remarks—known as the "Lyceum Speech"—are an important Lincoln text, containing clues about the developing mind of the future president. Lincoln was writing in a period when many Americans feared that vigilantism and mobocracy threatened their society. Lincoln's speech, titled "The Perpetuation of Our Political Institutions," still has relevance today:

> [L]et every man remember that to violate the law, is to trample on the blood
> of his father, and to tear the character of his own, and his children's liberty.
> . . . Let reverence for the laws, be breathed by every American mother, to the
> lisping babe. . . . Let it be taught in schools, in seminaries, and in colleges.
> . . . In short, let it become the political religion of the Nation.

┇☞THE YOUNG MEN'S LYCEUM will meet at
the usual time and place. In compliance with the request
of the Lyceum, A. LINCOLN, Esq. will deliver an
Address to the members of that body on Saturday evening
the 27th inst. The public are invited to attend.
By order of the Lyceum. J. H MATHENY, Sec'y.

Sangamo Journal *advertisement of Lincoln's speech to the Young Men's Lyceum*

33. LINCOLN'S CARRIAGE MAKER

LINCOLN BROUGHT HIS BUGGY TO OBED LEWIS FOR SERVICING

at his shop on the north side of Monroe Street between Sixth and Seventh Streets. When Lincoln first arrived in Springfield riding a borrowed horse, he wondered at the *"great deal of flourishing about in carriages"* he saw here. Eventually he could afford to buy his own. A lawyer friend recalled that Lincoln's blacksmith-made buggy was *"a most ordinary looking one."* Maintenance included occasional tire and floor repairs, repainting, and "oiling" the carriage top. The year before he ran for president, Lincoln had Lewis hang new interior silk curtains by glass hooks to the edge of the carriage roof. Lincoln also purchased a $7.00 wheelbarrow from Lewis and a $30.00 sleigh for winter transport. In 1852 Lincoln had Lewis replace his old buggy with a new carriage for $260—but a week later he brought it back for repairs! The next day he exchanged his new carriage for yet another. Even Lincoln, it seems, was not immune from buying an occasional "lemon."

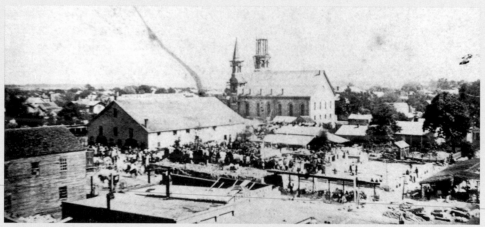

The American House Livery Stable was on the southwest corner of Seventh and Monroe Streets. Here guests at Springfield's most prestigious hotel boarded their animals while visiting Springfield. The workshop of Lincoln's carriage maker, Obed Lewis, is in the foreground.

HORSES WERE AN IMPORTANT

part of Lincoln's Springfield world. They provided locomotive power, carrying riders, pulling wagons and carriages—and producing manure that often piled up around the stables. Flies abounded and the stench could at times be stifling. One in twenty of Lincoln's neighbors worked with horses for a living, as teamsters, saddlers, wagonmakers, horse dealers, or liverymen. In town it was illegal to *"gallop"* a horse. An ordinance also forbade flying kites in the city for fear of spooking horses. *"Putting a stallion to a mare"* brought a $5 fine for *"indecent exhibition of horses."* Lincoln used city hay markets instead of gas stations; carriage shops instead of auto repair garages; stables instead of parking lots. He didn't have to buy licenses or liability insurance.

SPRINGFIELD COACH FACTORY.

H. VANHOFF & O. LEWIS.

NOTICE.—The subscribers informs their friends and the public, that they manufacture and keep on hand all description of Carriages. Having been engaged for several years in the above business, they feel conscious that their work for durability, neatness of execution and cheapness, cannot fail to suit those wishing to purchase. They have on hand several Buggies and Barouches, which they invite the public to call and examine. Their shop is opposite the Methodist Meeting House.

☞ They will also attend to the Waggon making business, and repairing of every description at the shortest notice. V. & L.

Springfield, April 10, 1840.—tf

Coach factory advertisement

A photograph from the 1890s shows Obed Lewis in his senior years, sporting a cane and reclining in a chair, while visiting with another old-timer, Roland W. Diller, who owned a drug store frequented by the Lincolns.

34. MARY LINCOLN'S FUNERAL

Elaborate floral decorations are prominent in this sketch of Mary Lincoln's funeral. "If her pathway was thorny, her journey to the grave was upon a bed of flowers," wrote one observer. Arrangements included a Book of Life inscribed "Mary Lincoln," a Gates Ajar, a tea rose pillow inscribed "From Citizens of Springfield," a Standing Cross and Anchor, and a Star of lilies above the pulpit—fitting tributes to Mary, who loved flowers.

MARY LINCOLN WAS THE FIRST

of the Todd sisters to die. At the age of sixty-three she succumbed to a variety of ailments that had filled her final years with physical torment. Her funeral was in the First Presbyterian Church on July 19, 1882. Mary's only surviving son, Robert, and her sisters Elizabeth, Frances, and Ann led mourners. Government offices and businesses closed for the funeral. The crowd overflowed from the church into the street. In a lengthy funeral oration the Rev. James A. Reed eulogized Mary and Abraham Lincoln as two "stately pines" so closely intertwined that when lightning struck and killed the one, the other lingered in slow death from the same cause. Mary had been a member of the First Presbyterian Church more than two decades earlier when the congregation occupied a different building. Church members brought the Lincoln family pew here, however, when they constructed this building in 1871, thus maintaining a Lincoln connection.

SPRINGFIELD'S CHURCHES WERE

torn over the slavery issue. Among the nineteen churches listed in the city's 1860 directory, opinions on slavery varied dramatically. Ministers who favored abolition supported Lincoln. But they were a minority. Unlike most northern-state ministers, many of Springfield's clergymen feared that Lincoln and the Republicans were too radically antislavery. Churches nationwide profoundly shaped popular and political culture in Lincoln's America. Evangelical Protestants in particular wielded strong cultural influence—and politicians responded by appealing to voters' religious sensibilities. Before the 1860 presidential election, Lincoln reportedly confided to a friend, *"Here are twenty-three [Springfield] ministers of different denominations, and all of them are against me but three; and here are a great many prominent members of churches, a very large majority of whom are against me."* Indeed, Lincoln lost the vote in his home county.

The First Presbyterian Church, circa 1872. Today tall spires no longer grace the church's towers.

35. THE CHILDREN'S LINCOLN

Neighbor girl Josie Remann was a favorite of Lincoln's. Once, on finding her in tears in front of her house, Lincoln ran all the way to the train station with her trunk on his shoulders because a carriage driver failed to come for it on time.

CHILDREN SEEMED NATURALLY fond of Abraham Lincoln, and he of them. *"He had a rare insight into boy nature,"* related a former neighbor boy. He took uncommon pains to remember their faces and names. He told them whimsical stories. He patiently answered their questions and encouraged their natural curiosity. When he took his boys to the circus he also took neighbor children along. Neighbors recalled seeing troops of children running out to meet Lincoln when he came home for dinner. They would *"gambol by his side,"* hold onto his long legs, and swing from his hands. Often he threw one of the smallest up onto his shoulder and gave the child a ride high above the others. Mischievous boys sometimes rigged a string across the street to knock the hat off Lincoln's head as he walked home. When Lincoln stooped to retrieve his hat, the young ambushers would jump from their hiding places and merrily mob their hatless neighbor. Lincoln would laugh at the joke and sometimes treat them to cakes and nuts.

To Lincoln's delight, Josie later married Mary Lincoln's nephew Albert Edwards, son of Ninian and Elizabeth Edwards.

BIRTHDAY PARTIES FOR CHILDREN

were not common in Lincoln's day. That didn't stop Mary Lincoln, however, from hosting a party in 1859 for her son Willie's ninth birthday. Mary was in the forefront of evolving nineteenth-century attitudes about childhood, the importance of the individual, increased age consciousness, and desires to instill proper social manners in children. Birthday parties in this period were formal affairs hosted in affluent homes by highly motivated mothers who invited many guests and personally attended to all details—from handwriting invitations to baking cakes to supervising activities. *"Some 50 or 60 boys & girls attended the gala,"* Mary reported. *"I have come to the conclusion that they are nonsensical affairs."* Neighbor boys like Isaac Diller may not have appreciated the formality of starched shirts and dress suits that etiquette required.

Mary gave her dead son Eddie's clothes to Josie's brother, Henry Remann. Lincoln sometimes joined Henry and others in games of marbles and ball, and in putting up swinging ropes. Henry corresponded faithfully with his long-time friend Willie Lincoln while Willie lived in the White House.

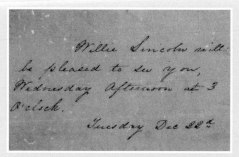

Invitation to Willie's birthday party in Mary Lincoln's hand

Neighbor boy Isaac Diller

36. MARY LINCOLN'S FAMILY

MARY FIRST VISITED SPRINGFIELD IN THE SPRING OF 1835.

She and her sisters were reared in Lexington, Kentucky, members of a prominent Kentucky family. Their mother died when Mary was six. One by one the four oldest Todd sisters left home, refugees from a difficult stepmother. Mary's oldest sister, Elizabeth, married Ninian W. Edwards, the son of an Illinois governor, and settled in Springfield. Elizabeth invited each younger sister to join her, in turn, assuming the role of matchmaker. The four Todd sisters, their uncle Dr. John Todd, and their cousin, the dashing John Todd Stuart, were socially prominent and made up part of the aristocracy of early Springfield. By most accounts, Mary was warmer and more personable than her sisters. None

Elizabeth Edwards

Frances Wallace

Mary Lincoln

Ann Smith

Ninian W. Edwards

William Wallace

Abraham Lincoln

Clark M. Smith

The four oldest Todd sisters each married a Springfield man and established households within a few blocks of each other. Elizabeth was the oldest and became Mary's surrogate mother. Frances lived closest to Mary (through the block where the Grace Lutheran Church now stands) and was described by some as "taciturn, cold, and reserved." Mary was thought by her sisters to be impossible. She caused a rift by marrying a commoner without refinement or family pedigree. Ann was the youngest. Mary resented surrendering her double name, "Mary Ann," when her younger sister was born.

shared her interest in public affairs. They all opposed her marriage to Abraham Lincoln, thinking she was marrying beneath herself. Elizabeth's matchmaking was more successful for her other sisters. The second oldest, Frances, married William Wallace, a physician and druggist who became the Lincolns' doctor. The youngest, Ann, married Clark M. Smith, a leading Springfield merchant.

THE TODD SISTERS FORMED A FEMALE SUPPORT NETWORK DURING

their early years of marriage and child raising. They could be jealous and competitive and sometimes quarreled. Relations were strained during the Civil War when the Todd family's Kentucky roots created political difficulties for the First Lady and her husband. The rift widened when a conflict arose with Elizabeth's husband over a government position. Nevertheless, family bonds were strong. Elizabeth went to Washington to be with Mary after Willie Lincoln died in the White House. In the last years of Mary's life, Elizabeth became her advocate, welcoming Mary back to Springfield to spend her last days in the Edwardses' home.

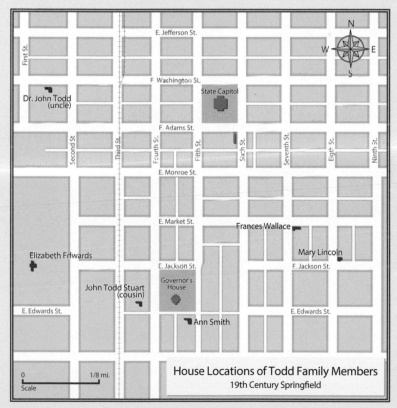

Mary Lincoln had three sisters, an uncle, and a cousin who lived within a few blocks of her in Springfield.

37. LINCOLN'S HORSE

SIMPLE CHORES HAD IMPORTANT CULTURAL SIGNIFICANCE

for men in Lincoln's day. A neighbor reports that Lincoln *"kept his own horse—fed and curried it,—fed and milked his own cow."* It was customary for men of all stripes to care for horses, but for those from Southern backgrounds (which in pre–Civil War Illinois was the majority—including Lincoln) milking was strictly women's work. In following the New England custom of men milking, Lincoln reflected a willingness to adopt "Yankee" attitudes that some of his Southern neighbors found degrading. No one could fault him on

When Confederate general Robert E. Lee surrendered to Union general Ulysses S. Grant at Appomattox Court House, Virginia, on April 9, 1865, joyous citizens decorated Lincoln's horse, Old Bob, with flags and led him triumphantly through the streets of Springfield. A week later, on April 14, Lincoln was shot and died the next day. On May 4 Old Bob was again decorated—this time in a black mourning blanket—and marched through Springfield for the last time as part of his former owner's funeral procession. Here Old Bob stands in mourning garb in front of the family home on Jackson Street.

cultural grounds, however, over horses. His bodyguard claimed Lincoln was *"passionately fond of fine Horses."* His opponents ridiculed his appearance in the saddle as being awkward. But Lincoln was apparently a skilled rider. He matched the horsemanship of dashing Gen. George B. McClellan at troop reviews during the Civil War—much to the general's dismay. And years after Lincoln was dead, no less an expert on horsemanship than Gen. Ulysses S. Grant proclaimed that Lincoln was indeed *"a fine horseman,"* having easily handled Grant's own mount, Cincinnati.

LINCOLN "LOVED HIS HORSE WELL." SO SAID LINCOLN'S NEXT-DOOR

neighbor, James Gourley. Lincoln owned several horses over the years—Tom, Belle, Old Buck, and finally Robin, whom Lincoln nicknamed "Old Bob" to distinguish him from his son Robert, "Young Bob." Old Buck and Old Bob, in particular, spent long hours plodding across many miles of Illinois prairie during the years when their owner was a circuit-riding lawyer. A fellow lawyer once described Lincoln riding to court *"behind his own horse, which was an indifferent, raw boned specimen."* This was probably Old Buck, as others described Old Bob as a *"pretty horse"* of *"bright reddish brown."*

> STRAYED OR STOLEN,
>
> FROM a stable in Springfield, on Wednes-day, 18th inst. a large bay horse, star in his forehead, plainly marked with harness, supposed to be eight years old; had been shed all round, but is believed to have lost some of his shoes, and trots and paces. Any person who will take up said horse, and leave information at the Journal office, or with the subscriber at New-salem, shall be liberally paid for their trouble.   A. LINCOLN.

When Lincoln visited Springfield in 1836, his horse strayed or was stolen. It is not known if he got it back. He was still a resident of New Salem at the time.

TREATMENT OF ANIMALS IN LINCOLN'S ERA SOMETIMES

reflected rough frontier attitudes. Pioneers saw them as threats to crops, gardens, and livestock; wild game was an important source of food. Lincoln, however, did not share the passion for hunting and fishing common to his generation. Nor did he often participate in such pursuits as cockfighting, gander pulling (wringing the head off a live goose), or cooking wild pigs alive. His stepmother said he generally loved animals and *"treated them kindly."* Stories

Exotic animals invaded Springfield whenever the circus came to town. Lincoln enjoyed taking his sons to see the animal menageries. This inspired young Bob and his friends to play "lion tamer" by having dogs stand on their hind legs and growl like lions. When the dogs refused, the boys proceeded to tie their front paws to a shed rafter, causing the dogs to sound a noisy alarm. Mr. Lincoln came running to the rescue—barrel stave in hand—and the would-be young showmen scattered.

illustrating this attitude abound. He once saved a piglet by beating its mother who was trying to eat it. Another time he passed by an old hog mired in the prairie mud. Compelled to look back, he seemed to hear it sigh, *"There now! my last hope is gone."* Guilt-stricken, he returned and freed it. Several lawyers were once riding across the prairie with Lincoln when he astounded (and amused) them by spending the better part of an hour searching for the nest of two baby birds who had been blown out during a windstorm.

THE LINCOLNS HAD THEIR SHARE OF PETS. LITTLE EDDIE, IN PARTICULAR,

loved kittens—a trait shared with his father. Mary joked that cats were her husband's "hobby." The boys used to harness dogs and cats to small wagons and drive them around Springfield's dirt streets or out into the woods to collect nuts. When the Lincolns left for Washington, D.C., in 1861, they had to leave their dog Fido behind. Fido stayed with the John Roll family, who, like the Lincolns, had young boys. One of the boys later recalled,

> One day the dog, in a playful manner put his dirty paws upon a drunken man sitting on the street curbing [who] in his drunken rage, thrust a knife into the body of poor Fido. . . . So Fido, just a poor yellow dog, met the fate of his illustrious master—Assassination.

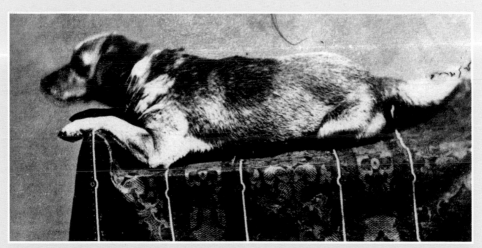

The Lincolns' dog, Fido

39. GREAT WESTERN RAILROAD DEPOT

MONDAY MORNING FEBRUARY 11, 1861, DAWNED DISMAL AND
gray. A chilling drizzle soaked the dirt roads of the capital. At 7:30 a carriage pulled up in front of the depot, and President-elect Lincoln climbed out. He found hundreds of well-wishers waiting in the rain. Inside the depot he shook hands. Lincoln reentered the street shortly before eight. Onlookers respectfully parted to the right and left as he walked to a train car a few yards north of the depot. He stopped on the rear car platform, took off his hat, and addressed the people of Springfield for the last time. A witness wrote, *"Many eyes were filled to overflowing. . . . [Lincoln's] own breast heaved with emotion and he could scarcely command his feelings sufficiently to commence."* The *Illinois State Journal* reported, *"We have known Mr. Lincoln for many years . . . but we never saw him so pro-foundly affected, nor did he ever utter an address which seemed to us so full of simple and touching eloquence. . . . God Bless honest Abraham Lincoln."* The whole affair from Lincoln's arrival to his departure took no more than thirty minutes.

Constructed in 1848, the Great Western Railroad Depot was a single story high in Lincoln's day.

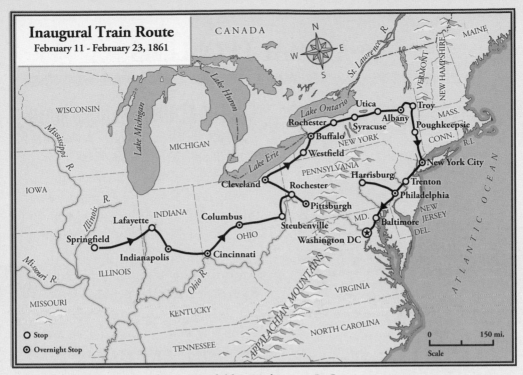

The inaugural train route from Springfield to Washington, D.C.

LINCOLN'S INAUGURAL TRIP TO WASHINGTON, D.C., WAS FRAUGHT

with danger. In the South secessionists were establishing a new government and arming for war. In Washington rumors abounded of secessionist plots to seize the capital city. In Springfield Lincoln was receiving death threats. Secretary of State designee William Seward pled with Lincoln to come to Washington *"by surprise—without announcement."* Not since George Washington's first inaugural trip from Mt. Vernon to New York City in 1789 had an American president made such a dramatic, public journey prior to assuming office. So why did Lincoln overrule caution and begin a twelve-day roundabout itinerary that took him through seven states with overnight stops in nine major cities? He never specifically said. Historians speculate that he hoped his trip would rally support for the Union.

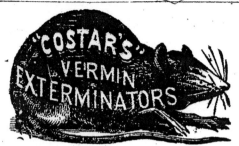
Rats and mosquitoes were consequences of urbanization, according to a nostalgic local editor, who in 1859 lamented, "It is a little singular that Springfield was never annoyed by the presence of a rat or a mosquito, until after the railroads were built to the place. Now in both respects, the town is becoming quite citified."

CULTURAL DIFFERENCES MADE it hard for citizens to agree on animal control policies. Well into the 1850s hogs freely roamed the streets, contesting the walkways with pedestrians, rooting up sidewalk planks, and creating smelly "hog wallows" in front of stores. Attempts by middle-class reformers to pass ordinances requiring owners to keep hogs penned routinely failed. Opponents, usually Southerners and poor immigrants, argued that scavenging pigs cleaned dirty streets and enabled poorer people to raise their own meat. Dogs were also a nuisance. Roving packs foraged in the streets. "Mad dog" scares were common. People generally ignored licensing laws. The city marshal was criticized for "murdering" thirty dogs in an 1851 campaign against strays. Yet a few years later others complained that "500 to 1,000 worthless curs in Springfield" threatened the health and safety of the citizens. Prairie wolves were yet another concern. As late as 1845 citizens engaged in "wolf hunts" on the outskirts of town. Men on horseback chased the wolves down and dispatched them with strong hickory clubs.

ALARMED WHEN YOUNG ROBERT LINCOLN

was bitten by a dog thought to have rabies, Lincoln hurried Bob all the way to Terre Haute, Indiana, to find a "madstone" that, when applied directly to a bite wound, was supposed to "suck out the poison." Madstones were usually hairballs or rocks formed of calcium deposits from the guts of animals. Regarding Lincoln's belief in mad-stones, his friend Joseph Gillespie once wrote,

> *He had great faith in the strong sense of Country People and he gave them credit for greater intelligence than most men do. . . . He had great faith in the virtues of the mad stone, although he confessed that it looked like superstition. But he said he found the People in the neighborhood of these stones fully impressed with a belief in their virtues from actual experiment and that was about as much as we could ever know of the properties of medicines.*

As a child, Robert Lincoln was bitten by a dog thought to have rabies.

"Madstones" such as this were thought to cure rabies.

41. REPUBLICAN WIGWAMS

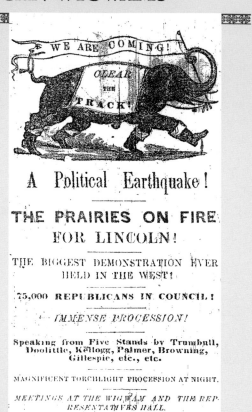

Newspaper notices from the 1860 presidential campaign advertising events at Springfield's "Wigwam"

DURING THE 1860 ELECTION,

Illinois Republicans held conventions in temporary wood-and-canvas structures dubbed "Wigwams." Wigwams were reminiscent of the "Log Cabins" from the 1840 presidential campaign. They quickly became symbols of the young Republican Party's vigor. Cheap, easy to construct, commodious, and conducive of generating party spirit, they made ideal political assembly halls. *"Every Republican club in every considerable town will have its wigwam,"* party leaders boasted. In Decatur's Wigwam state Republicans nominated

Lincoln for the presidency. In Chicago's two-story, wood-frame Wigwam the country's Republicans nominated Lincoln as their national candidate. Springfield Republicans had a Wigwam, too. Erected on the southeast corner of Sixth and Monroe Streets, Springfield's Wigwam was a circular or octagonal frame structure, 90 feet in diameter, with a high pitched roof, wide interior gallery, wooden benches, and a sawdust floor. It could seat 3,000 people. On numerous occasions during the summer and fall of 1860 local party leaders and distinguished out-of-towners whipped the party faithful to a frenzy. Candidate Lincoln visited on occasion, but following the tradition of his day he *did not* give a campaign speech there—or anywhere else.

DURING THE CIVIL WAR THE STATE OF ILLINOIS BUILT A SOLDIERS'

Home where the Wigwam had stood. Used as a barracks and a receiving station for sick soldiers, its second-floor balcony was filled with cots, and on the ground floor were offices, a kitchen, dining room, and a room where women of the Ladies' Soldiers' Aid Society made bandages, splints, and other first aid items. The U.S. government owned the corner lot on which the Home was built. President Lincoln authorized its use for a Soldier's Home *"with the understanding that the government does not incur any expense."* When invited to attend the dedication in April 1864, the President had to send his *"regrets."* War matters were too pressing to permit a trip home to Springfield.

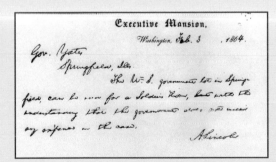

Lincoln's February 3, 1864, letter authorized construction of a Soldiers' Home on federally owned land.

Illinois' wartime governor Richard Yates, a Republican ally of Lincoln's, stands in front of the Soldiers' Home during the Civil War, wearing a Lincoln-like stovepipe hat.

Whigs parading in the 1840 "hard cider" campaign. They cast President Van Buren as an effete dandy and General Harrison as one of the common people. The sign on the keg of cider says, "Van drinks wine but Old Tippecanoe drinks Hard Cider."

POLITICS IN LINCOLN'S DAY

was a heady mixture of civic duty and community entertainment. A striking example of mid-19th-century hoopla was the gigantic Whig rally and parade held during the 1840 presidential campaign. Whigs supported Gen. William Henry Harrison against the incumbent Democrat, Martin Van Buren, in the "log cabin and hard cider" campaign. Whig faithful converged on Springfield from as far as 200 miles in all directions. Veterans of the Revolution and the War of 1812 led the parade. Soon came Illinois delegations. *"First among these was the Cook County contingent with a miniature brig, thirty feet long and completely rigged, drawn by six white horses. Fayette County had a log cabin which its delegates had dragged all the way from Vandalia . . . bands were plentiful, banners myriad."* Up and down Sixth Street marched the delegates. When they reached the prairie at the south end of town, they *"marched, counter-marched and cheered themselves hoarse . . . [then] headed north again."* On the north end of town 15,000 people were served an *"old style barbecue."* Hard cider was plentiful.

THIRTY-ONE-YEAR-OLD ABRAHAM

Lincoln was an ardent Whig in 1840. An eye-witness observed his role in these proceedings:

> *Mr. Lincoln stood in a wagon, from which he addressed the mass of people that surrounded it. . . . At times he discussed the questions of the time in a logical way, but much time was devoted to telling stories to illustrate some phase of his argument, though more often the telling of these stories was resorted to for the purpose of rendering his opponents ridiculous. . . . One story he told . . . was not one it would be seemly to publish; but rendered, as it was, in his inimitable way, it contained nothing that was offensive to refined taste.*

Faint praise for the man who, in the maturity of his later years, would become his nation's most eloquent spokesman for its most cherished political ideals.

An 1840 political poster announcing a meeting to prepare for the pro-Harrison parade and convention to be held in Springfield on June 4

Political campaign items on display at the Abraham Lincoln Presidential Museum

Wide-wakes wore unique uniforms—dark caps and capes covered with glazed cloth that protected them from hot oil splatters from the torches they carried in nighttime parades.

WHEN LINCOLN RAN FOR

president in 1860, young Republican men across the country formed semi-military clubs called "Wide-Awakes." Wide-Awakes led spectacular night-time torchlight parades. "Privates" carried torches, while "officers" carried colored lanterns. They marched in cadence to martial music, performed precision drills, and sang uproarious campaign songs. Their *"flickering lights"* passed *"like a fiery dragon as far as one could see."* Besides marching, Wide-Awakes distributed campaign literature, escorted speakers, and policed rallies. On Election Day they monitored voting lines, challenged suspicious voters (in those days voters did not preregister), and checked to see that Republican ballots were genuine before they were cast. Douglas Democrats countered by forming their own clubs with names like the "Ever-Readys," "Little Giants," "Little Dougs," or "Douglas Invincibles." One such group—the "Chloroformers"—vowed to *"put the Wide-Awakes to sleep!"*

SPRINGFIELD'S WIDE-AWAKES INVITED ALL OTHER ILLINOIS

Wide-Awakes to attend the statewide Republican "ratification" rally set for August 8, 1860. A procession of farm wagons, carriages, riders, floats, flags, banners, and bands noisily rolled past Lincoln's home on Jackson Street from morning until evening, and was said to stretch for eight miles. The night brought fireworks, and more than 2,000 Wide-Awakes marched past midnight. *"As far as the eye could reach . . . a seemingly interminable line of flame stretched out its moving length,"* remarked a reporter. The June 1840 Springfield Harrison rally had been the benchmark for large political gatherings until the 1860 Lincoln rally.

Parade participants had their photograph taken in front of Lincoln's home during the August 8, 1860, "ratification" rally. Lincoln is the tall, white-coated figure near the doorway. Mary peers from the bottom far left window. Today the Lincoln Home is open to visitors as a National Historic Site administered by the National Park Service.

44. MASONIC HALL

MASONIC LODGES WERE AMONG the most important local social institutions of Lincoln's day. They reflected the "associational culture" of the time. People formed all sorts of groups to address local concerns and to foster collective improvement. Fraternal societies in particular were important for constructively channeling the attention and energies of young single men who had few ties to the community. The Springfield Masonic Lodge was

A spacious Masonic Hall was erected in 1853 (top left) and enlarged in the 1860s (inset above). Springfield suffered a great loss when it burned down in 1871. In Lincoln's time the Hall served as an important public facility. The Masons let it out for many events— political gatherings, "Practicing Parties" (dances), pageants, plays, band concerts, lectures, and various fund-raising dinners (Mary Lincoln is known to have participated in some). Well-known opera singers, violinists, guitar players, and Shakespearean readers performed here. It housed the state's geological collection for a time, and in 1855 the local postmaster moved the post office to a room in the lower level.

chartered in 1839. Stephen Douglas joined. Lincoln did not. When later asked about it, he allegedly replied, *"I feared I was too lazy to do all my duty as I should wish to were I a member."* When asked to join after his election as president he reportedly said he would be *"charged with wrong motives,"* and deferred the matter *"to some future time."* He surely visited the Masonic Hall occasionally, however. For Lincoln was fond of oysters—and in the Hall's basement was Lanihan's Restaurant, which featured oysters and wild game *"served in best style, and on the shortest notice."*

Early Springfield settler and Masonic leader James Adams

JAMES ADAMS WAS INSTRUMENTAL

in founding Springfield's Masonic Lodge. He later served as Masonic deputy grand master for Illinois. He was an early Springfield settler, arriving in 1821 from upstate New York. He practiced law, speculated in land, and was a militia leader. As a leading Democrat he helped in the early career of Stephen Douglas. In 1837 Adams ran for probate judge against Lincoln's friend Anson Henry. Young Lincoln viciously attacked Adams's integrity in a scathing series of anonymous letters published in the local Whig newspaper. Adams protested and won despite the attacks. Perhaps the antipathy between the two men is one reason Lincoln didn't join the Masons when the Springfield Lodge was chartered in 1839. Adams did not live to see the new Masonic Hall. He joined the Mormons and died at Nauvoo in 1843.

Many of Lincoln's contemporaries were Masons. Lincoln was not.

45. LEAPING LINCOLN

Joseph Gillespie

Asahel Gridley

IN NOVEMBER 1840 LEGISLATORS convened in the cramped quarters of the Methodist Church while workers were completing the statehouse a block away. *"The House of Representatives was crammed in a room barely large enough for the members to turn round in, having no tables to write upon, or space to move from one part of the house to another,"* newspapers reported. These conditions added to the confusion Lincoln encountered as leader of the minority Whig party. On December 5, when the Democratic majority was about to pass a measure that threatened the State Bank, Whigs conspired to prevent a legal voting quorum by staying away. Only Lincoln and a few lieutenants remained to observe. Suddenly it became evident that Democrats had rounded up enough members to form a quorum. *"Mr. Lincoln came under great excitement,"* Democrats mocked. Blocked from the

Fellow Whig legislators Joseph Gillespie and Asahel Gridley joined Lincoln in leaping from the Methodist Church window in an ill-fated attempt to stop a legislative vote. "We have not learned whether these flying members got hurt," wrote bemused Democrats; Lincoln, they assumed, had not "as it was noticed that his legs reached nearly from the window to the ground!" Democratic editors suggested that workers add a "third story" to the new statehouse "so as to prevent members from <u>*jumping out of the windows!*</u> *. . . Mr. Lincoln will in [the] future have to* <u>*climb down the spout!*</u>*"*

door, he *"unceremoniously raised the window and jumped out."* The Democratic measure passed anyway. An embarrassed Lincoln ever after resented references to what he called that *"jumping scrape."*

NO PICTURES EXIST OF THE WOOD-FRAME METHODIST CHURCH THAT

stood from 1831 to 1854. A visitor described it as *"a modest-looking meetinghouse, which speaks more for the simple piety of the inhabitants, than the ostentatious taste of the citizens."* The state legislature, circuit court, and private schools also used the building. But the old church eventually proved too small. In 1854 members dedicated a new brick building with seating capacity for 500. The graceful $700 spire blew down, however, during a violent storm—*"a rebuke from the Lord for the extravagance and pride of the Methodists of Springfield in these latter days,"* declared the Rev. Peter Cartwright (hence, the "spireless" picture).

The old wood-frame Methodist Church from which Lincoln "leaped" was replaced in 1854 by the brick structure reflected in this 19th-century lithograph.

46. VIRGIL HICKOX HOME

This 1902 photo is the oldest known picture of the Hickox home. Hickox built it in 1839 and enlarged it several times afterwards. It is the oldest single-family residence still standing on its original foundation in downtown Springfield. Hickox died in 1880, but the home's notoriety as a political hangout continued. It housed Springfield's first private men's club; during Prohibition there was a "speakeasy" in the basement. From Lincoln's time to the present, many prominent Illinois politicians have congregated there.

VIRGIL HICKOX WAS ONE OF MANY LOCAL PEOPLE WHO

disagreed politically with Abraham Lincoln. Raised in the traditions of Jeffersonian Democracy as a youth in New York, he settled in Springfield in 1834 and became a prosperous merchant, railroad promoter, and banker. He was an important supporter of Stephen Douglas. Republicans attacked him during the 1858 senatorial contest for having his railroad company provide Douglas with a private train car for use in his statewide canvas against Lincoln. *"Huge corporations . . . [are making] electioneering machines of themselves,"* critics complained. Hickox insisted that the arrangement was not free (Douglas reportedly spent $50,000 on the Senate campaign—a tremendous sum in those days; some of it probably compensated the railroad). Hickox was among the Sangamon County majority that opposed Lincoln in 1858 and in both presidential elections (Lincoln never carried his home county in these contests). Politics didn't prevent Lincoln and Hickox from enjoying cordial professional relations, however. *"I have always found Mr. Hickox a fair man in his dealings,"* Lincoln once wrote a law client.

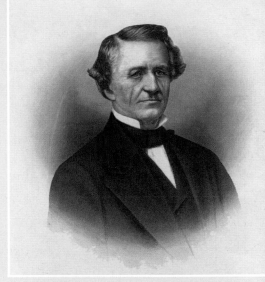

Virgil Hickox

STEPHEN DOUGLAS'S FAMOUS

last letter—dated May 10, 1861—was addressed to Virgil Hickox, chairman of the state's Democratic Central Committee. Hickox worried that Democrats were confused by Douglas's apparent flip-flop in support of Lincoln's military response to Southern secession. Hickox warned that previous Douglas speeches had conditioned Democrats *"to believe that Mr. Lincoln has no constitutional right to pursue his present course."* In what is apparently the last letter Douglas ever wrote, he denied becoming a Republican apologist, and reminded the party faithful *"that a man cannot be a true Democrat unless he is a loyal patriot."* Hickox counseled Douglas to keep the letter private pending further events. But Douglas's father-in-law ignored Hickox's instruction and published it anyway. Douglas died soon thereafter. His parting sentiments helped solidify Northern support behind Lincoln at the start of the Civil War.

Stephen A. Douglas

47. CLARK AND ANN SMITH HOME (VACHEL LINDSAY HOME)

Ann and Clark Smith bought this house from the Rev. Charles Dresser (who also married the Lincolns and later sold them their own house). The Smiths owned this property from 1853 to 1865. Their oldest child, ten-year-old Clark Jr., died of typhoid fever in this house just four weeks after his uncle was nominated for the presidency. Mary came and helped Ann during most of the boy's last week. "I trust never to witness such suffering ever again," Mary wrote a friend. But just two years later she did indeed again witness such suffering when her own son Willie died in the White House. Today the Smith Home is administered by the Illinois Historic Preservation Agency and is interpreted as the home of early-20th-century poet Vachel Lindsay.

JEALOUSY SOMETIMES MARRED relations between Mary Lincoln and her younger sister Ann. Ann's sentiments reflected those of some in Springfield who were chagrined that Mary's uncouth husband had ascended to the highest office in the land, leaving other local worthies behind. Taking cruel aim at her sister in the White House, Ann gossiped that Mary was conducting affairs like *"Queen Victoria's Court."* Her feelings wounded, Mary never invited Ann to Washington. She wrote bitterly of Ann's *"miserable disposition"* and *"false tongue"*—saying, *"I grieve for those who have to come in contact with her malice."* In childhood Mary had resented all the attention little Ann received from older relatives after the death of their mother. Ann's talent in sewing and embroidery (she often won awards at agricultural fairs) exceeded Mary's. Mary also came to distrust Ann's husband, businessman Clark M. Smith, calling him *"silly & malicious."* Simmering jealousies notwithstanding, the Clarks reportedly hosted the Lincolns on their last evening in Springfield. For years afterward, several of Ann's German house servants would boast of having cooked for the future president in this house.

"YEA, LINCOLN—HOW HE HAUNTETH

us!" wrote Vachel Lindsay. When Lincoln appears in Lindsay's poems, he is usually a dematerialized persona appropriated for emotional symbolism to underscore poetic themes. *"Would I might rouse the Lincoln in you all,"* the poet declared in the twenty-fourth stanza of "Litany of the Heroes" (1907–8), in which Lincoln embodies the wild prairie—*"Born where the ghosts of buffaloes still gleam."* Lindsay's most famous Lincoln treatment—"Abraham Lincoln Walks at Midnight" (1914)—was one of five poems the poet frantically penned in a single day at the outbreak of World War I. In it, Lincoln is a grieving presence in *"suit of ancient black"* pacing the dark night streets of his hometown without rest, longing for an end to war—*"That he may sleep upon his hill again."*

Vachel Lindsay (1879–1931)—one of Illinois' "Prairie Poets" of the early 20th century

Ann Smith, sister of Mary Lincoln, and her husband, Clark M. Smith

48. ILLINOIS EXECUTIVE MANSION

ABRAHAM LINCOLN NEVER SERVED AS GOVERNOR OF ILLINOIS.

He was very involved, however, in the administration of Illinois' first Republican governor, William Henry Bissell. Bissell, a former Democrat whose anti-slavery views placed him at odds with his old party, was popular among voters for his military valor during the Mexican War and for challenging Jefferson Davis (future Confederate president) to a duel when the two men served together in the U.S. Congress (the duel was averted). Bissell won election despite an illness that confined him to a wheelchair. Bad health forced him to run the government from his room in the Mansion rather than from the

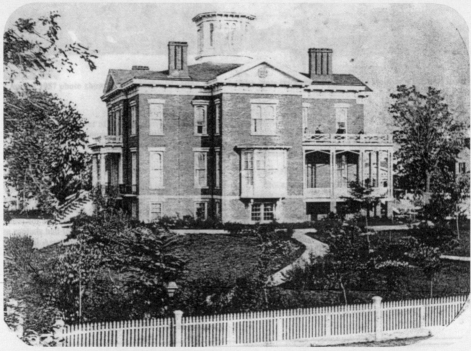

Of the five men who resided in this house as governor during Lincoln's lifetime, all but one (Joel Aldrich Matteson) were Republican colleagues of the Civil War president. When Gov. William Henry Bissell died in March 1860, Lt. Gov. John Wood stayed at his home in Quincy after taking over the duties of governor, permitting the Bissell family to remain in the Mansion until Governor Yates moved in following the 1860 election. Previous to the construction of the Executive Mansion at this location, governors lived in a much more modest house on the northwest corner of Eighth and Jackson Streets—just a block north of Lincoln's home.

governor's office in the Capitol building. Lincoln was a frequent visitor—so
much so that he was acknowledged
as the governor's "special advisor."
He helped Bissell write his inaugural
address; he drafted veto messages;
he defended the governor before the
Illinois Supreme Court when Bissell
tried to void a bill he had accidentally
signed into law. Lincoln was among
those whom Bissell summoned to his
deathbed the day before he died in the
Mansion on March 18, 1860.

WILLIE AND TAD LINCOLN

reportedly once climbed onto the Mansion roof through a bedroom window of
one of Governor Bissell's daughters, terri-
fying onlookers below before anxious staff
members could retrieve them. Twelve-
year-old Robert Lincoln was more re-
strained than his younger brothers when
he and other Springfield young people
"hopped about" at a special youth dance
hosted here by Governor and Mrs. Matteson. Abraham and Mary Lincoln were
likely among the many who received an
invitation from the Mattesons to attend a
housewarming here in January 1856. The
Lincolns, like other curious city residents,
would have witnessed the progress of
construction beginning in the summer
of 1853 and running through November
1855. Not being an avid hunter, Lincoln
was probably not bothered that state officials built the new Executive Mansion in
the middle of Cook's Grove—a favorite
hunting spot for locals.

*Mexican-American War hero William
Henry Bissell—the first Republican
governor of Illinois (1857–60)—was an
invalid throughout his term in office.*

*Mathew Brady took this photograph
the day Lincoln gave his Cooper
Union Speech in New York City, just
a few weeks before Governor Bissell
died in Springfield.*

49. NINIAN AND ELIZABETH EDWARDS HOME

"I WANT TO GET HITCHED TONIGHT," declared Abraham Lincoln to the startled Rev. Charles Dresser at the minister's Friday morning breakfast on November 4, 1842. Mary Todd's relatives were even more startled—and upset—at Mary's sudden Friday morning announcement. For several years Mary had been living with her sister and brother-in-law, Elizabeth and Ninian Edwards. Most members of the Todd and Edwards families considered Lincoln a "plebeian" and strongly opposed the match. When it became clear that the marriage would take place immediately regardless of family sentiments, the Edwardses insisted that the ceremony be held in their home. Stressed by inadequate time to prepare for the event, Elizabeth complained that she would have to buy *"some gingerbread and beer"* from a local confectionary. Mary tartly replied, *"Well, that will be good enough for plebeians, I suppose."* In the end, Elizabeth successfully hosted about thirty friends and relatives that evening as Abraham and Mary exchanged vows in her parlor. While cold rain rattled the windows, guests enjoyed slices of warm wedding cake—a tribute to Elizabeth's frantic last-minute preparations.

Elizabeth Edwards, sister of Mary Lincoln, and her husband, Ninian Edwards

"I FEEL LIKE I AM BEING HACKED TO PIECES,"

complained an ailing Mary Lincoln. Suffering from an
injured spine, chronic kidney problems, cataracts, and
probably diabetes, Mary could no longer live alone. So
she returned here to the home of her sister Elizabeth.
She rented four rooms on the second floor. In two rooms
she stored sixty-four trunks of cloth goods. Floorboards
groaned under the weight. The maid feared being in
the room beneath. Mary spent hours poring over the
contents of her trunks. Other times she simply sat
quietly in her shuttered room, her eyes closed (blinking
was excruciatingly painful—the result of swollen corneas
caused by excessive weeping). Children passing by wondered aloud about the "crazy lady" living upstairs in the
Edwardses' home. Mary died in this house of a stroke on
July 16, 1882. She was sixty-four.

*The Edwards home, shown here in an early image, was an important social center in Lincoln's
Springfield. At the time the Lincolns were married there, the house stood aloof from the
community of Springfield, which lay off at a distance. But by the time Mary Lincoln died there
forty years later, the city had totally engulfed the area and the elegant, old Edwards home was
completely overshadowed by the edifice of the newly constructed capitol building.*

50. MATHER'S GROVE

ABRAHAM LINCOLN WOULD HAVE BEEN BURIED WHERE THE
capitol building now stands had Mary Lincoln not intervened. Political and
business leaders hoped to inter the martyred president somewhere in Springfield close to the railroad and local businesses. Without consulting Lincoln's
widow, a committee purchased the Mather lot for $5,300, quickly constructed
a temporary vault, and began plans to erect a monument there. Mary objected
as soon as she heard. She insisted it had been her husband's desire that his remains rest *"in some quiet place"*—she wanted him buried outside town amidst
"the beauty & retirement" of the rural Oak Ridge Cemetery. Her opposition
set local people *"in a rage."* According to one observer, *"All the hard stories that
ever were told about [Mrs. Lincoln] are told over again. She has no friends here."*
But Mary's determination was "unalterable." She threatened to move Lincoln's
body to the vault originally prepared for George Washington under the dome
of the national capitol if her wishes were not followed. Officials relented and
Lincoln was laid to rest in the serenity of Oak Ridge Cemetery.

*In Lincoln's day this area was known as "Mather's Grove"—six acres of elevated land
covered largely by beautiful stands of native trees that surrounded the imposing stone home
of the Thomas Mather family. Just days after Lincoln's assassination, Springfield citizens
bought this property and hastily constructed a vault they hoped would hold the president's
remains until a larger monument could be built. The vault was never used. In 1868 the
State of Illinois acquired the lot and began construction of the current capitol building.*

At Mary's insistence, Lincoln was buried in the countryside at Oak Ridge Cemetery. Today the Lincoln Tomb State Historic Site is open to visitors and administered by the Illinois Historic Preservation Agency.

CASSIUS CLAY SPOKE IN MATHER'S

Grove on July 10, 1854, while on a speaking tour attacking Stephen A. Douglas's Kansas-Nebraska Act. State officials barred the controversial Clay from speaking as scheduled in the rotunda of the Old State Capitol. A large crowd followed him here and listened to his two-and-a-half-hour speech under the grove's canopy of trees. Clay was a friend of Mary Lincoln's from her Lexington childhood. Years later, Clay wrote that Abraham Lincoln lounged on the grass whittling sticks while patiently listening to Clay's *"animated appeals for universal liberty."* Clay flattered himself that his speech *"sowed [the] seed which in due time bore fruit"* in the future president's wartime crusade against slavery. It is true they shared a conviction that the Declaration of Independence applied to blacks as well as to whites.

Kentucky abolitionist Cassius Clay

ALSO OF INTEREST
FOR FURTHER READING
ILLUSTRATION CREDITS
INDEX

ALSO OF INTEREST

THE ABRAHAM LINCOLN PRESIDENTIAL LIBRARY AND MUSEUM
provides a one-of-a-kind introduction to the life of America's sixteenth president. The Library houses the world's largest collection of materials created by, owned by, or about the Lincolns. The Museum has an array of exhibitions and special-effects theatrical presentations that immerse visitors in Lincoln's nineteenth-century world. Together, the Library and Museum serve as the gateway to Illinois' many other Lincoln-related historic sites and visitor attractions.

Museum Plaza

Nine-year-old Lincoln in Indiana

Lincoln family

Cabinet room

Lincolns at Ford's Theater

Historian with Lincoln's ghost

FOR FURTHER READING

Angle, Paul M. *"Here I Have Lived": A History of Lincoln's Springfield.* Chicago: Abraham Lincoln Book Shop, 1971.

Burlingame, Michael. *The Inner World of Abraham Lincoln.* Urbana: University of Illinois Press, 1994.

Hart, Richard E. *Lincoln's Springfield: The Public Square, 1823–1865.* Springfield, Ill.: Elijah Iles House Foundation, 2004.

Randall, Ruth Painter. *Lincoln's Animal Friends.* Boston: Little, Brown, 1958.

———. *Lincoln's Sons.* Boston: Little, Brown, 1955.

Wilson, Douglas L. *Honor's Voice: The Transformation of Abraham Lincoln.* New York: Knopf, 1998.

Winkle, Kenneth J. *Abraham and Mary Lincoln.* Carbondale: Southern Illinois University Press, 2011.

———. *The Young Eagle: The Rise of Abraham Lincoln.* Dallas: Taylor Trade Publishing, 2001.

ILLUSTRATION CREDITS

All maps were created by Tom Willcockson of Mapcraft Cartography specifically for this book. All other images in this book are courtesy of the Abraham Lincoln Presidential Library and Museum (a division of the Illinois Historic Preservation Agency), except for the following:

Institutional Repositories

- Library of Congress—watercolor of coast of Liberia (American Colonization Society Collection), p. 11; Mary Lincoln and close-up of her hand, p. 20; Sarah Rickard Barret, p. 39; 1840 campaign parade, p. 86; public meeting poster, p. 87; Stephen A. Douglas, p. 95.
- Lincoln Financial Foundation Collection, courtesy of the Indiana State Museum and Allen County Public Library—Thomas "Tad" Lincoln, William Wallace "Willie" Lincoln, and Robert Todd Lincoln, p. 9.
- Looking for Lincoln Heritage Coalition, courtesy of Sarah Watson—Larry Anderson's Statue Grouping, p. 7; Lincoln-Herndon Law Office State Historic Site, p. 49; Lincoln Tomb State Historic Site, p. 103.
- Meserve-Kundhardt Foundation—Isaac Diller, p. 73; Frances Wallace, p. 74.
- National Museum of Health and Medicine, Silver Spring, Md.—madstone, p. 83.
- Sangamon Valley Collection, Lincoln Library, Springfield, Illinois—Baptist church, p. 66; Springfield landscape with Masonic Hall inset, p. 90.

Public Domain Publications

- *Ballou's Pictorial Drawing-Room Companion*, November 15, 1856—"View in Washington Street, Springfield, Illinois," p. 5.
- *Frank Leslie's Illustrated Newspaper*, April 14, 1860—John C. Heenan, p. 59.

- *Illinois State Journal*—(December 23, 1854, 2:5) Christmas advertisement, p. 8; (August 1, 1844, 2:1) campaign flag pole, p. 26; (December 1, 1860, 2:5) Heenan reception advertisement, p. 59; (May 25, 1860, 2:5) firemans' ball advertisement, p. 65; (August 1, 1860) "Lincoln and Hamlin" advertisement, p. 84; (August 9, 1860) "We are Coming" advertisement, p. 84.
- *Illinois State Register*—(November 2, 1858, 3:3) "People of Sangamon . . ." advertisement, p. 24; (November 3, 1858, 2:2) "Sangamon for Douglas!" advertisement, p. 25; (October 4, 1854, 1:4) Corneau & Diller newspaper advertisement, p. 57; (September 3, 1841, 1:1) Florville barbershop advertisement, p. 63; (April 10, 1840, 3:6) coach factory advertisement, p. 69; (March 25, 1864, 2:5) rat trap advertisement, p. 82.
- Lane, Richard James, *Life at the Water Cure; or, A Month at Malvern: A Diary . . . to Which Is Added a Sequel* (London: Longman, 1846), 190—bathtub, p. 11.
- *Sangamo Journal*—(December 1, 1838, 2:6) American House advertisement, p. 60; (April 13, 1843, 4:1) fire engine advertisement, p. 65; (January 27, 1838, 2:7) lyceum advertisement, p. 67; (June 17, 1837, 2:3) "Menagerie and Circus United" advertisement, p. 78.
- *Springfield City Directory for 1857–'58*, p. 74—dental advertisement, p. 14.
- *1863 Springfield City Directory*, p. 50—billiard hall advertisement, p. 43.

INDEX

BRYON C. ANDREASEN is a historian at the LDS Church History Museum in Salt Lake City, Utah. Previously he was a research historian at the Abraham Lincoln Presidential Library and Museum in Springfield, Illinois, where he curated exhibits and conducted seminars and other public programming. The author helped create the Looking for Lincoln Heritage Coalition, a 501(c)3 corporation that pioneered heritage tourism in Illinois, and he authored the feasibility study on which Congress based legislation creating the Abraham Lincoln National Heritage Area. For ten years he was the editor of the *Journal of the Abraham Lincoln Association*, the premier scholarly journal in the field of Lincoln studies.